Victorian Ghosts in the Noontide

VANESSA D. DICKERSON

Victorian Ghosts

in the Noontide

WOMEN WRITERS AND
THE SUPERNATURAL

UNIVERSITY OF MISSOURI PRESS
COLUMBIA AND LONDON

Library of Congress Cataloging-in-Publication Data

Dickerson, Vanessa D., 1955–
    Victorian ghosts in the noontide : women writers and the
supernatural / Vanessa D. Dickerson.
        p.   cm.
    Includes bibliographical references (p.   ) and index.
    ISBN 0-8262-1081-3 (alk. paper)
    1. English fiction—Women authors—History and criticism.
2. Supernatural in literature.   3. Women and literature—Great
Britain—History—19th century.   4. English fiction—19th
century—History and criticism.   5. Ghost stories, English—
History and criticism.   I. Title.
PR878.S85D53   1996
823'.80937—dc20   96-27410
                                                                 CIP

∞™ This paper meets the requirements of the
American National Standard for Permanence of Paper
for Printed Library Materials, Z39.48, 1984.

Designer: Mindy Shouse
Typesetter: BOOKCOMP
Printer and binder: Thomson-Shore, Inc.
Typefaces: Minion and Shelley

For Yanna and a cat

9897-b

Contents

ACKNOWLEDGMENTS

I WOULD LIKE to thank U. C. Knoepflmacher for believing in ghosts. I would also like to thank the Faculty Development Committee at Rhodes College for providing money that allowed me to complete research for two of the chapters. I am grateful to Mary Lago for her thoughtful reading of the manuscript and to Ellen Armour for suggestions she offered on Irigaray and Brontë. Annette Cates deserves thanks for arranging untold numbers of interlibrary loans; I owe thanks to Chuck Wilkinson for his help with the bibliography. Finally, I am grateful to Beverly Jarrett and Jane Lago for their wisdom and their professionalism.

Victorian Ghosts in the Noontide

INTRODUCTION

$\mathcal{A}$T 124 BLUESTONE Road, Sethe, the protagonist of Toni Morrison's *Beloved,* joins hands with her daughter Denver, and the two summon the spirit of the infant girl who has been haunting their home. "Come on. Come on," they chant; soon enough, the dead child does just that.[1] *Beloved* is a bold book because it treats its ghost seriously in the face of a twentieth-century skepticism arrogant in its assumptions about the correctness, power, and truth of its empiricism, technology, and materialism. When Sethe allows the ghost of her child access to her house and life, she not only invites the return of the repressed but also demonstrates a more universal willingness of the female to readmit that which the dominant culture officially casts out.

Morrison's use of folkloric and supernatural elements in her novels *Song of Solomon* and *Beloved* constitutes an act not only artistically, historically, and spiritually inspiring, but one also as practical and satisfying as that of the woman who takes the discarded scraps and pieces of old dresses, shirts, sheets, and bedspreads, then stitches them into a quilt of recovery. After all, the summoning of the ghost in *Beloved* was a natural if not a logical step for Morrison, who has admitted that

1. *Beloved,* 4.

1

the supernaturalism of her fiction is integral to a "cosmology" she knew because she grew up in a house where people dreamed, "talked about their dreams," and "had visitations." She is anything but apologetic for a traditional African American belief in ghosts and spirits when she asserts, "My own use of enchantment simply comes because that's the way the world was for me and for the black people that I knew. In addition to the very shrewd, down-to-earth, efficient way in which they did things and survived things, there was this other knowledge or perception, always discredited but nevertheless there, which informed their sensibilities and clarified their activities." The ghost of *Beloved* comes out of Morrison's people, her culture, and finally her courage, for to write about the supernatural is risky business: one may not be taken seriously. As deconstructionist Shoshana Felman reminds us, "The 'supernatural,' as everyone knows, cannot be rationally explained and hence should not detain us and does not call for thought." In a world where "an ideological conditioning of literary and critical discourse, a political orientation of reading," results in a "censorship mechanism" that describes "an inside that is *inclusive* of 'reason' and men, 'reality' and 'nature'; and an outside that is *exclusive* of madness and women, that is, the 'supernatural' and the 'unreal' "—in such a world, it is not only the female characters but also and especially the very writings of women about the supernatural that are susceptible to being "flattened out and banalized."[2] In a society where women are traditionally associated with unreason, emotion, even hysteria, a woman writing about ghosts and spirits may be at a distinct disadvantage.

Toni Morrison's reappropriation of the supernatural in her contemporary novel bears an interesting relation to a similar phenomenon in the works of the white, mainly middle-class Victorian women who are the subject of this study. Although these women differ in terms of their race, geographical location, and place in time, they share Morrison's impulse to reclaim what has been discredited. Like Morrison, they acknowledge and concern themselves with spirit. Like Morrison, these women wrote about the supernatural in spite of societies that were likely to be more resistant to women than to men who explored, employed, or accepted supernatural beliefs.

2. Christina Davis, "Interview with Toni Morrison," 414, 415, 414; Felman, *What Does a Woman Want? Reading and Sexual Difference,* 30, 29, 30. Felman's brief glance at the supernatural occurs in the chapter of her book called "Women and Madness."

This last point of intersection between a contemporary black female writer and white British Victorian female writers—the resistance to or the discouragement of women who treat supernaturalism—is a compelling point of engagement, especially since this work, *Victorian Ghosts in the Noontide,* aims itself critically to recover and highlight the supernaturalism of writers including Charlotte and Emily Brontë (1816–1855; 1818–1849), George Eliot (1819–1880), and Elizabeth Gaskell (1810–1865) through rereadings of well-read or relevant texts. After all, the fact is that acts of recovery, especially those involving the supernatural, are fraught with peril for the woman writer, be she novelist or critic. In a study of women, folklore, and the supernatural that was published the same year as Toni Morrison's *Beloved,* Gillian Bennett comments that "though it takes some courage to say so . . . of all types of folklore, this [supernatural folklore] is the one that seems *least* respectable and *least* believable in a so-called scientific age." Bennett goes on to give three reasons that the supernatural and its recovery are problematic. First, no one, she observes, wants to address the subject because it is "disreputable," and "it remains disreputable because no one will tackle it." Second, since no one researches today's supernatural beliefs, "occult traditions" are stuck in a "time-warp" wherein they are still perceived in terms of "legends about fairies, bogeys, and grey ladies." Finally, Bennett observes that no one is willing to talk about their supernatural experiences, so there is little evidence for the supernatural, and since there is little evidence no one is willing to talk about it. Ghosts, spirits, and folklore are the stuff of "old-wives' tales, superstitions, fallacies, legends and quaint customs that linger on in backward country areas and provide evidence of outmoded belief-systems and pagan religion." Consequently, for a woman to embrace supernaturalism in an age defined by science, technology, and materialism suggests a kind of intellectual and cultural suicide. "By withdrawing to the more occult or esoteric realms," notes Sally Gearheart, acknowledging a modern-day concern about women's spirituality, "we yield up to men the real world, the world of power and excitement and achievement."[3] This observation, doubly meaningful for Toni Morrison as a black, female, contemporary writer, is also of special

3. Bennett, *Traditions of Belief: Women and the Supernatural,* 13, ix; Gearheart, "Womanpower: Energy Re-Sourcement," in Charlene Spretnak, ed., *The Politics of Women's Spirituality: Essays on the Rise of Spiritual Power within the Feminist Movement,* 201. Even men who saw ghosts lost privilege, for ghost-seeing in Victorian England was neither a masculine nor a real feat. Jennifer Uglow, in

relevance to Victorian women, who were among the very first to find themselves in an increasingly mechanized universe.

Factories, railroads, Corn Laws, poorhouses, and doctrines of evolution all evinced the materialism, skepticism, and empiricism that rapidly altered the Victorian world. In this time of great technological, scientific, and economic changes, engineered for the most part by men such as Watt, Bentham, Darwin, and Huxley, women's lives were powerfully affected. Shortly after the turn of the century, the feminist author of *African Farm,* Olive Schreiner, observed in her landmark work *Woman and Labour* that one of the significant ways in which these changes ultimately affected woman was to diminish her contribution, and I would add her socially perceived connection, to the "material conditions of life": "The changes which have taken place during the last centuries, and which we sum up under the compendious term 'modern civilisation,' have tended to rob woman, not merely in part but almost wholly, of the more valuable of her ancient domain of productive and social labour; and, where there has not been a determined and conscious resistance on her part, have nowhere spontaneously tended to open out to her new and compensatory fields."[4]

Robbed of place, of space, of substance in a society that, after Carlyle, defined work as harmony, nobility, sacredness, self-knowledge, and life, the Victorian woman paled in the real, the material, the business world. By the nineteenth century, of course, the shifting of woman from out-doors where she toiled in the fields to indoors where she no longer even spun, wove, or brewed to sustain the family and its coffers had been effected. The ideal woman was now to attend to the physical, moral, and spiritual needs of the family as the angel in the house. One of the things expected of Victorian woman, as mother, wife, and daughter, was that she control herself and suppress desire and passion, as these would be disruptive to her mission as stabilizer of the home. It was mete that woman give up, rein in, be silent, be still. She was to fulfill "her role by disappearing into the woodwork to watch over the household," by becoming a ghost. Bound as she was by domestic and cultural ideology, she was yet allowed the valve of her own spirituality. However, just as

---

her introduction to *Victorian Ghost Stories by Eminent Women Writers,* notes that "the experience of seeing a ghost pushes men into conventional female roles: timid, nervous, helpless" (xvii).

4. *Woman and Labour,* 50.

surely as woman's spirituality was part of her reverenced angelic status, it was also a part of her denigration in an age in which, as Victorian writer, translator, and editor William Howitt commented, "The tendency of both philosophy and general education for more than a century has been, whilst striving to suppress all prejudice, to create a load of prejudice against everything spiritual."[5]

Further and further removed from the power-wielding occupations of the world—law, science, medicine, even the formal administration of religion—yet relegated to the higher realm of moral influence, the position of the nineteenth-century female, as influential as it was, was yet equivocal, ambiguous, marginal, ghostly. Indeed, women were "powerful and peripheral." Striking as it is, this paradox finds a most interesting expression in women's relations to the supernatural, particularly the ghost, a figure of indeterminacy, of imperiled identity, of substance and insubstantiality. Although the figure of the ghost bespoke a general discomfort with the interstices opened up by rapid technological change, economic and political reform, and "religious life . . . intense and disputatious," the ghost corresponded more particularly to the Victorian woman's visibility and invisibility, her power and powerlessness, the contradictions and extremes that shaped female culture.[6] Little wonder that in Victorian England women could and did discover in the supernatural some of those "new and compensatory fields" Schreiner mentions, not only playing key roles in the popularizing of such phenomena as mesmerism and spiritualism, but also contributing to the tremendous output of ghost stories that provided a counter to the scientism, skepticism, and materialism of the age.

While an account of why the female writers considered here were attracted to the supernatural may begin with national ghosts or with

5. Carlyle, "Labour"; Nancy Armstrong, *Desire and Domestic Fiction: A Political History of the Novel*, 80; Howitt, "Letter," in *Report on Spiritualism of the Committee of the London Dialectical Society, Together with the Evidence Oral and Written, and a Selection from the Correspondence*, 236.

6. Catharine R. Stimpson, foreword to *Independent Women: Work and Community for Single Women, 1850–1920*, x. See also Diana Basham's *The Trial of Woman: Feminism and the Occult Sciences in Victorian Literature and Society*, in which she notes that the ghost had "much in common" with Victorian women, "for both ghosts and women were subject to the same kind of criticism and liable to be met with the same dismissive hostility in their attempts to gain recognition" (151–52). What Basham does not acknowledge is the emancipatory aspect of the ghost, its duality, its betweenness. Robin Gilmour, *The Victorian Period: The Intellectual and Cultural Context of English Literature, 1830–1890*, 63.

the age's own haunted zeitgeist, that same account must go beyond mere period anxiety to touch upon more basic questions of identity, of expression, of place, of what it means to be that which Simone de Beauvoir has called "the second sex." Noting that the removal of women from certain areas of experience could only mean that avenues of expression that had once been open to them were blocked off, Schreiner, who concedes that "several women of genius in modern times have sought to find expression for their creative powers in the art of fiction," promptly explains how this phenomenon is not necessarily evidence of "some inherent connection in the human brain between the ovarian sex function and the art of fiction." She has it that fiction writing for women is an outlet.

> The fact is, that modern fiction being . . . the only art that can be exercised without special training or special appliances, and produced in the moments stolen from the multifarious, brain-destroying occupations which fill the average woman's life, they have been driven to find this outlet for their powers as the only one presenting itself. How far otherwise might have been the directions in which their genius would naturally have expressed itself can be known only partially even to the women themselves. . . . Even in the little third-rate novelist whose works cumber the ground, we see often a pathetic figure, when we recognise that beneath that failure in a complex and difficult art, may lie buried a sound legislator, an able architect, an original scientific investigator, or a good judge.

If, as Schreiner states, writing stories is an outlet for the energies of woman, the act of writing a ghost story was for the popular woman writer the creation of a public discourse for voicing feminine concerns.[7]

In singling out these concerns in the fictions of nineteenth-century British women writers, I neither mean to suggest that the supernaturalism of Victorian men is not as compelling nor to imply that it is essentially ghost-free. It is, however, different. This is to say that, though both men and women write ghost stories, they do them in different

7. See de Beauvoir's *The Second Sex;* Schreiner, *Woman and Labour,* 158–59; studies such as Basham's *Trial of Woman,* Howard Kerr's *Mediums, and Spirit-Rappers, and Roaring Radicals: Spiritualism in American Literature, 1850–1900,* and Alex Owen's *The Darkened Room: Women, Power and Spiritualism in Late Victorian England* connect women's participation in the occult to radical movements such as suffragettism and feminism. These works do not, however, focus on women's expression of and concerns about indeterminacy, displacement, in-betweenness.

voices. Thus, the supernatural tales by such representative writers as Sheridan Le Fanu, Charles Dickens, Edward Bulwer Lytton, and Robert Louis Stevenson—writers whose ghost stories have received the lion's share of critical attention—tend to be more diagnostic, clinical, journalistic, vested in mensuration.[8]

Of the male writers who wrote supernatural stories, Henry James came closest to experiencing the in-betweenness of the female writer, though his is one that finally "reflects a threatened masculinity." As David McWhirter points out in an essay in which he actually concludes with a recognition of James's "in-betweenness," "Henry James was a sexually ambivalent man, probably homoerotically inclined, who grew up in a family where he was often assigned the role of 'sissy,' and in a society that defined his very vocation as part of a feminized cultural sphere." James's "uncertainties about his own masculinity" tended to align him with femaleness; nevertheless, James himself, as McWhirter points out, regarded supernatural texts like *The Turn of the Screw* not only as "mere experiments" but also as "fictions" that "were slight affairs because they were implicitly 'feminized' " or, as James says specifically of *The Turn of the Screw,* "wanton little text[s]." Even James, then, perceived himself to be operating, to borrow Shoshana Felman's words, at the "so-called objective level" by experimenting with, if not meeting, the patriarchally constructed "norms of 'legibility.' "[9]

Unconsciously or not, Victorian men wrote their tales in assurance: the male writer of ghost stories wrote from the hegemonic position in a society in which the masculine ways of knowing, thinking, and doing were automatically acknowledged as best, more reasonable than those of women who, as angelic nurturers and homemakers, did not often get ranked among the great thinkers and rationalists of the day. Even though the nineteenth-century male writing a supernatural story was not entirely exempt, he was less likely to incur the charge of engaging in "the

---

8. Good examples of these tendencies in men's ghost stories are Le Fanu's "Green Tea," with its medical sleuth, Dr. Hesselius; Dickens's "The Signalman," with its haunted technologized space, the railroad; and Stevenson's *The Strange Case of Dr. Jekyll and Mr. Hyde,* with its mixture of medicine and the supernatural. These stories and others like them have been examined in such works as Julia Briggs's *Night Visitors: The Rise and Fall of the English Ghost Story,* Jack Sullivan's *Elegant Nightmares: The English Ghost Story from Le Fanu to Blackwood,* and Peter Penzoldt's *The Supernatural in Fiction.*

9. McWhirter, "In the 'Other House' of Fiction: Writing, Authority, and Femininity in *The Turn of the Screw,*" 142, 126, 125, 126; Felman, *What Does a Woman Want?* 29.

frivolous amusement of unrigorous minds." For while these men were
readily enough seen as men at play, as men dabbling in the supernatural
and the arcane, their play, having more ballast or rigor, even tended
toward what would in some later male writers of supernatural tales be
identified as antiquarianism.[10] It was finally not men's but women's ghost
stories that truly treated the return of the repressed and the dispossessed;
ghost stories could provide a fitting medium for eruptions of female
libidinal energy, of thwarted ambitions, of cramped egos.

Indeed, as a mode that treats the meeting, the confrontation, the
connection of opposites and the phenomenon of suspended being,
the ghost story proved especially attractive to Victorian female writers,
whose society, as I have indicated, not only found in the female Coventry
Patmore's "angel in the house" but also made of her a tightly corseted
body that, set loose, could prove not just uncomely but, according to
Nina Auerbach, the very devil.[11] In the séance room, at the mesmeric
session, but particularly in the ghost story, woman could more freely
and safely examine the possibilities and limitations of her mythical role
as the angel in the house, and she could, if she chose, release those not
so angelic impulses, feelings, and desires that the age publicly denied
her. Victorian women's participation in the revival of supernaturalism,
whether as mesmeric subjects, as mediums, or as writers of ghost stories,
constituted both expression and exploration of their own spirituality and
their ambiguous status as the "other" living in a state of in-betweenness:
between the walls of the house, between animal and man, between angel
and demon.

By investigating Victorian women's contributions to the supernatural
furor and debate that was as much a component of the age as its railroads
and reform bills, this work specifically aims to do a combination of three
things. First, it will define the sociocultural and historical context of
women's supernatural writings. Next, it will shed more light on Victorian
ideas about women's spirituality. Finally, it will offer specific readings of

---

10. Karen Chase, *Eros and Psyche: The Representation of Personality in Charlotte Brontë, Charles
Dickens, and George Eliot,* 55; see Sullivan, *Elegant Nightmares,* 69–111.

11. Nina Auerbach examines the inverse of the angel—the demon—in *Woman and the Demon:
The Life of a Victorian Myth.* Though Auerbach does an excellent job of discussing the "mermaids,
serpent-women, lamias" that were expressions of popular myth, she overlooks the ghost, an even
more compelling manifestation of the "energy of the uncanny" (8, 9).

women's supernatural fictions. These readings, which are the core of the book, are not meant to demonstrate that Victorian women all wrote the very same ghost story; instead, they are meant to describe a grouping, if not limn a tradition, of women's supernatural fiction that addresses issues of gendered energies and spirituality, of power and powerlessness, of women's precarious position on the continuum of materialism and spiritualism, of women's visibility and invisibility, of what amounts to the in-betweenness of ghosts.

The first two chapters lay the groundwork for subsequent readings of the supernatural fiction of four major Victorian women writers. Chapter 1 identifies the unique supernatural revival that took place during the Victorian period and determines how the supernatural so shaped and was shaped by Victorian men in the vanguard of intellectual, technological, and material progress that the figure of the ghost became a period metaphor. Huxley, Arnold, Carlyle, Cruikshank, Lang, and others are co-opted in the examination of how ghosts, phrenology, mesmerism, and spiritualism related to Victorian science, religion, and culture. Chapter 2, which draws out the special connection between women and ghosts, focuses exclusively on women who participated in the supernatural revival through séances, mesmeric sessions, and nonfiction writings about the subject. As this chapter's title, "A Spirit of Her Own," indicates, the supernaturalism of this period afforded women an unprecedented opportunity to explore for themselves the nature of the culturally granted spirituality that gave them a power or influence that was limited to the domestic sphere.

The next three chapters focus on women's supernatural fiction published during the 1850s, specifically that of Charlotte and Emily Brontë, George Eliot, and Elizabeth Gaskell. The supernatural works of these women are of great interest because these writers were prominent and successful, in their day standing apart from the record number of women like Mrs. Henry Wood, Ella D'Arcy, Rosa Mulholland, Dinah Mulock Craik, Margaret Oliphant, Amelia Edwards, and Charlotte Riddell who also wrote ghost stories during the nineteenth century. Another reason for considering these particular writers is that they are not as quickly associated with the supernatural as are popular writers such as Charlotte Riddell, who is termed by E. F. Bleiler "the best distaff writer of ghost stories" and the one who came "closest to being a specialist in the form," or even writers such as Margaret Oliphant, whose book-length ghost story *Beleaguered City* rivals her domestic fiction in being one of her best-written works and her personal favorite. What Michael Cox and R. A. Gilbert identify as "one of the great unasked critical questions"—"why women took to the ghost story so successfully"—is more compellingly addressed in the works of women writers not noted for such productions. What could induce a woman writer in an age so earnestly worshipful of and dedicated to the pursuit of intellectual and material progress, one, moreover, convinced that women intellectually and materially had and could have little to offer in this, the real and material world—what could so move a woman writer such as Mary Ann Evans, known to her readers as George Eliot, to indulge in the supernatural and risk becoming one of the "outcasts of the establishment of readability"?[12] What use did she make of it?

The final chapter considers works written after the 1850s by popular women who often were not only "feeding the periodical mind,"[13] as Bleiler puts it, but also literally feeding their families and themselves with the proceeds from the sale of these stories. Writers such as Margaret Oliphant, Charlotte Riddell, and Florence Marryat, this chapter shows, wrote ghost stories that tended to center on money and supernaturalism, though these writers did not abandon the earlier women writers' focus on the seesaw of women's energies and powers.

From the Brontës to Marryat, the women writing stories of the supernatural were engaged in disclosing, re-creating, and examining not just the cultural but also the gendered paradox, the equivocal position that constituted their own special brand of ghosthood. At a time when nineteenth-century men pushed on to greater and greater heights in science, technology, and administration, women were expected to ground and center this progress, to be fulcrums for the disequilibrium of change. Although they were not required to go backward, they were not encouraged to go forward into the exchange, laboratory, courtroom, classroom, or, for that matter, the bedroom. The supernatural fictions of such Victorian women writers as the Brontës, George Eliot, Elizabeth

---

12. Bleiler, in Charlotte Riddell, *The Collected Ghost Stories of Mrs. J. H. Riddell,* ed. E. F. Bleiler, v; Cox and Gilbert, eds. *Victorian Ghost Stories: An Oxford Anthology,* xiv; Felman, *What Does a Woman Want?* 29.

13. *Collected Stories of Mrs. J. H. Riddell,* ed. Bleiler, xv.

Gaskell, Margaret Oliphant, Charlotte Riddell, and Florence Marryat are premier expressions, if not of a feminized limbo, then of woman's in-betweenness. As different as they and their works are, these women wrote supernatural stories shaped by and revelatory of an awareness that the Victorian woman was above all the ghost in the noontide, an anomalous spirit on display at the center of Victorian materialism and progress. Destined to be seen but unseen, required to shine forth in the broad daylight as an ethereal being, but thought to be too fleshy, too corrupt and corruptible, she lived during an era of the highest material, social, and political achievement, yet found herself all too often unable fully, if at all, to participate.

1

GHOSTS OF THE VICTORIANS

THAT PREEMINENT man of science and letters, T. H. Huxley, shook the supernatural dust from his feet on January 29, 1869, when he curtly declined the London Dialectical Society's invitation to consider the subject of spiritual manifestations. "I take no interest in the subject," he wrote. "But supposing the phenomena to be genuine—they do not interest me. . . . If any body would endow me with the faculty of listening to the chatter of old women and curates in the nearest cathedral town, I should decline the privilege, having better things to do." Huxley's peremptory if not combative missive belies the age's unique hauntedness. As Ronald Pearsall wrote in *The Table-Rappers,* "The Victorian period was not only a haunted age; it was also, in every sense of the word, a hallucinatory age, lending itself to every type of illusion, even at the level of bricks and mortar. . . . [There were] money boxes disguised as books, substantial looking doors that on examination was [*sic*] merely cunning paintwork, solid-looking chairs that were, in fact, featherlight, being manufactured from papier maché." Such furnishings, calling into question the very results of the mechanical accomplishments of the age, set the stage for the specters and ghosts whose place in and impact on the times proved just as substantial as any technological creation or advancement the age could boast. For one of the most interesting, if little appreciated, paradoxes of the Victorian period is that while it was the age of Darwin and Mill—an age that called for and prided itself on "Facts, sir; nothing but Facts!"—this same age was preoccupied with the supernatural, especially with the idea of ghosts.[1]

This is not to say that the Victorians had a monopoly on ghosts. As Gillian Bennett reminds us in *Traditions of Belief*, "Belief in occult forces is both endemic and ancient, one of the most enduring matters of interest." Yet the fact that the belief in ghosts is a primal and longstanding one does not controvert its special significance for the period. For in nineteenth-century England, the ghost figured as one of the cornerstones of what Alfred Russel Wallace—biologist, naturalist, and co-originator with Charles Darwin of the theory of evolution—in 1878 identified as "this revival of so-called supernaturalism," an acknowledgment of supernatural phenomena unparalleled "in the history of human thought; because there never before existed so strong, and apparently so well-founded a conviction that phenomena of this kind never have happened and never can happen." In *Cock Lane and Common Sense*, Andrew Lang, the Victorian man of letters best known for his work with fairy tales, also notes the nineteenth century's investment in ghosts. "In the Middle Ages—the 'dark ages'—modern opinion would expect to find an inordinate quantity of ghostly material," wrote Lang, "but modern opinion would be disappointed. Setting aside saintly miracles, and accusations of witchcraft, the minor phenomena [ghosts, clairvoyance, noises, and so on] are very sparsely recorded." Lang went on to observe with no little disdain that "the dark ages do *not*, as might have been expected, provide us with most of this material. The last forty enlightened years give us more bogles than all the ages between St. Augustine and the Restoration." A particularly compelling focus for the energy, ambivalence, and anxiety that typified the period, the ghost became, if not, in M. H. Abrams's words, a "period-metaphor," then, in Carlyle's even more appropriate coinage, one of the "signs of the times," a marker of social, historical, and philosophical positionality, an emblem of "the perplexed scene where we stand."[2]

---

1. Huxley, "Letter," in *Report on Spiritualism*, 229; Pearsall, *The Table-Rappers*, 139; Charles Dickens, *Hard Times*, 47.

2. Bennett, *Traditions of Belief*, 23; Wallace, *Miracles and Modern Spiritualism: Three Essays*, 54, 149; Lang, *Cock Lane and Common Sense*, 28, 30; Abrams uses the expression "period-metaphor" in

The ghost was after all a provocative, in some cases provoking, image not just for fiction writers such as Bulwer Lytton, Charles Dickens, and Robert Louis Stevenson, but also for other eminent Victorians who wrote to and about the times.[3] Thus, Matthew Arnold conjures up one of the most evocative nineteenth-century ghosts in the resounding and oft-quoted lines from "Stanzas from the Grande Chartreuse," a Victorian zeitgeist: "Wandering between two worlds, one dead, / The other power-less to be born."[4] This spectrally announced betweenness, a condition with which Victorians could identify, since they found themselves be-tween medieval god and modern machine, monarchy and democracy, religion and science, spirituality and materiality, faith and doubt, au-thority and liberalism—this condition of betweenness familiar to men would prove practically synonymous with the lives of Victorian women.

The dualities, tensions, and anxieties of a people so ambiguously situ-ated have been documented by scholars including Walter E. Houghton, who, noting the age to be a transitional one, determined that "never before had men thought of their own time as an era of change *from* the past *to* the future." Although the telling and apt designation of the age as a period of change, transition, and progress is no misconception, it proves imprecise if not problematic when applied to Victorian spiritu-ality, for in this arena the Victorians did not necessarily have a sense of moving on. They were caught between belief in the old order and faith in the new one evidenced in science and technology. Aware of this inertia, Houghton cites Carlyle, "The Old has passed away . . . but, alas, the New appears not in its stead; the Time is still in pangs of travail with the New."[5] At the intersection of a world dying if not dead and one all alive with potential though not yet born, the wonderings and wanderings of Victorians describe a condition of Arnoldian suspension and ambiguous animation that constitutes ghosthood. The figure of the ghost can represent very well the paradox of the Victorian frame of mind, touted for its utility and rationality, yet tenacious of its spirituality.

Natural Supernaturalism: Tradition and Revolution in Romantic Literature, 31; see Carlyle's "Signs of the Times" in *A Carlyle Reader*, ed. G. B. Tennyson, 34.

3. More recently Nina Auerbach has noted the ghost's relation to the theatrics of Victorian lives in *Private Theatricals: The Lives of the Victorians*.

4. *Poetry and Criticism of Matthew Arnold*, 187.

5. *The Victorian Frame of Mind, 1830–1870*, 1, 9.

When Charles Darwin published in 1859 one of the most definitive texts of the age of intellect, *The Origin of Species,* he strengthened the hand of science, which had been chiseling away at the concepts of miracle, creation, and supernaturalism. Ultimately, the onslaught of science, materiality, fact, and reason, which in the nineteenth century culminated in such works as Robert Chambers's *Vestiges of the Natural History of Creation,* Darwin's *Origin,* Huxley's "On a Piece of Chalk," and the Higher Criticism of the Bible, shook the church but only stirred up the ghosts (the gain in knowledge and understanding was great, but the loss in spiritual security was vexatious) as Darwin and other thinkers deprived the age of one of life's greatest miracles and exchanged the wondrous and purposeful workings of the universe for a law of natural selection that finally, as J. A. V. Chapple has commented, "seemed far more uncontrollable and random" than the scientific insistence on "law" indicated.[6]

As early as the 1830s, the Victorian prophet Thomas Carlyle would consider "with some half-visible wrinkle of a bitter sardonic humour" the scientific debunking of life's mysteries:

> Our Theory of Gravitation is as good as perfect: Lagrange, it is well known, has proved that the Planetary System, on this scheme, will endure for ever; Laplace, still more cunningly, even guesses that it could not have been made on any other scheme. Whereby, at least, our nautical Logbooks can be better kept; and water-transport of all kinds has grown more commodious. Of Geology and Geognosy we know enough: what with the labours of our Werners and Huttons, what with the ardent genius of their disciples, it has come about that now, to many a Royal Society, the Creation of a World is little more mysterious than the cooking of a Dumpling; concerning which last, indeed, there have been minds to whom the question, *How the apples were got in,* presented difficulties.

As Carlyle, posing as editor of *Sartor Resartus,* takes stock of the advances science has made in accounting for the workings of the universe, he disparages the self-congratulatory tone and the complacency, if not indeed the offensive confidence, underlying the scientific pronouncements about the nature of things. Yet, for all science's certainty about the

---

6. *Science and Literature in the Nineteenth Century,* 82.

"good as perfect" theory of gravitation, about a planetary scheme that "will endure for ever," and its confident guess that the planetary system "could not have been made on any other scheme"—for all its vaunted command of the facts and knowledge of the universe it cannot address the simple but profound question of how "*the apples* [the spark, the soul, the spirit of the universe] *were got in.*" While the efforts, discoveries, and inventions of scientists and men such as Darwin, Lyell, Huxley, Davies, Faraday, Watt, Arkwright, and Stephenson continued to demystify and mechanize the world with finitude, empiricism, and materialism that rendered life "little more mysterious than the cooking of a Dumpling," the apples to which Carlyle satirically refers were the Victorians' spiritual longing for the infinite, the inexplicable, the immortal, a longing that remained constant though now troubled.[7]

Carlyle, whose prose writings earned for him the holy status of prophet-seer, was keenly aware of and wrote aggressively about the relations between the old and the new, about the living miracle of the spiritual and the dead fact of the material. In one of his typically windy and passionate deliveries as *Sartor Resartus*'s Teufelsdröckh, Carlyle bridges the gaping chasm between spirit and fact with the figure of the ghost:

> Again, could anything be more miraculous than an actual authentic Ghost? The English Johnson longed, all his life, to see one; but could not, though he went to Cock Lane, and thence to the church-vaults, and tapped on coffins. Foolish Doctor! Did he never, with the mind's eye as well as with the body's, look round him into that full tide of human Life he so loved. . . . Are we not Spirits, shaped into a body, into an Appearance; and that fade away again into air, and Invisibility? This is no metaphor, it is a simple scientific *fact:* we start out of Nothingness, take figure, and are Apparitions; round us, as round the veriest spectre, is Eternity. . . . —Ghosts! There are nigh a thousand million walking the earth openly at noontide; some half-hundred have vanished from it, some half-hundred have arisen in it, ere thy watch ticks once.
>
> O Heaven, it is mysterious, it is awful to consider that we . . . are, in very deed, Ghosts!

7. *Sartor Resartus,* 25, 3. In *The Victorian Frame of Mind,* 110, Houghton, who writes about, among other things, the anti-intellectualism that was also afoot during the Victorian period, makes an important distinction between the scientific and intellectual mind versus the practical and mechanical mind that helps account for the complex relations of apparently antagonistic ideas of science and the supernatural.

In this passage Carlyle argues, in the words of George Eliot's Ladislaw, that "the true seeing is within." But blinded by the "shows of things," humankind must perforce live in "the very fact of things": human beings stop at the "Appearance" or "*vesture*" of things and so thereby miss the reality of the "divine mystery"—the ghost.[8] Carlyle reminds his readers of the realness of the unseen, averring that spirituality is a fact. He thus extends the bounds of reality with his use of the word *ghost*, a literalization of spirit.

While Carlyle appropriated the ghost as an emblem or avatar of an eternal reality, others tried to dispel or exorcise it as a figure of trespass. Some scientists were especially annoyed when, oddly enough, science itself became haunted. Through the quasi-scientific explanations that undergirded such phenomena as mesmerism and spiritualism, supernatural beliefs and old a priori truths were provided with an unlikely vehicle. Mesmerism, a phenomenon in which a controller made passes over some bodily part of a subject, rendering that subject liable to a trancelike and restorative sleep—this mesmerism, or animal magnetism, as it was called by its discoverer, "the founding father of modern hypnosis," Viennese doctor Franz Anton Mesmer (1734–1815), was based on the scientific concept of a magnetic field or Newtonian fluid surrounding all things in the universe.[9] This field could be tapped by magnetic individuals who then controlled certain responsive subjects. Mesmerism would in turn pave the way for the midcentury advent of spiritualism, as the same fluid that enabled one body to communicate energy and currents to another body also facilitated human communication with dead spirits.

Mesmerism itself had earlier in the nineteenth century been allied with another so-called science that preceded it: phrenology. During the early part of the nineteenth century, this quasi science, the basic theories of which were expounded by Franz Joseph Gall, identified in the brain over thirty propensities (including amativeness, acquisitiveness, secretiveness), sentiments (self-esteem, veneration, ideality), and intellectual faculties (individuality, language, causality) that could serve as the basis

8. Carlyle, *Sartor Resartus*, 200–201; Eliot, *Middlemarch*, 142; Carlyle, "The Hero as Poet. Dante; Shakespeare," 115.
9. E. R. Hilgard, introduction to *Mesmerism: A Translation of the Original Scientific and Medical Writings of F. A. Mesmer*, xi. For his ideas about fluids and fields, Mesmer relied largely on Newton's theory of the tides; he also relied on Volta and Galvini's work with magnets.

for the "analysis of mental character." Phrenology asserted that the brain was the center of both thought and feeling and that the size of different organs of the brain determined human behavior. Dr. John Elliotson, who sacrificed a medical chair at London University for his work with these fringe sciences, would be one of a number of adherents who tried to connect phrenology to mesmerism. But as Karen Chase points out in *Eros and Psyche,* her study of personality in three Victorian writers, the two "sciences" were an unlikely pair, "sharing little more than their hostility to established psychological theories."[10]

As a science, phrenology was more contained and centered in the physical than was mesmerism. Phrenologists had instruments they used to measure the head, providing among other things "the measure of an organ's power." The organs of the brain were intricately mapped and numbered. There was a comforting and more solid empirical dimension to this science than to that of mesmerism, whose main "instruments" were the touch or pass of a hand, the voice, the will, and an invisible magnetic field and fluids. On the one hand, the mesmeric "treatment necessary to restore the patient to harmony, with himself and with nature," as Janet Oppenheim observes, "had far more in common with the stroking, or laying-on of hands, practiced by faith healers and village wizards than with the standard eighteenth-century doctor's bag of frequently murderous medical tricks." On the other hand, as John D. Davies has pointed out in his text on phrenology in nineteenth-century America, *Phrenology: Fad and Science,* phrenology had a utilitarian dimension that members of society in Britain as well as in America must have found appealing:

> Phrenologists told their age how to be happy, how to choose a pro-fession, how to select a wife, how to raise children; not only did they maintain that education was of supreme importance but they offered detailed curricula and pedagogical techniques. Other socio-logical and psychological applications were the diagnosis and cure of insanity, the conduct of penology, and the reform of the criminal. . . . Finally, for the common man, who did not understand philosophy, psychology, or physiology, phrenology afforded a "scientific" method of character analysis, aptitude testing, and vocational guidance. This

10. George Combe, *Notes on the United States of North America during a Phrenological Visit in 1838–9–40,* 1:xviii; Chase, *Eros and Psyche,* 105–6.

young, experimental, and somewhat protean science was of interest to
scientists, doctors, social thinkers, and reformers of every description;
and for those persuaded by its optimistic and utilitarian interpretation
of life it offered hope for all and a vision of ultimate perfection.

It is not that mesmerism and spiritualism did not also proffer utopian
ideas of perfectibility, but whereas phrenology provided detailed answers
for daily living, mesmerism's and spiritualism's more spiritual provisions
and promises were neither so immediate nor so concrete; they were
supernatural. Phrenology, however, appeared to be, as John Purkis has
observed, "the conclusion of a chain of reasoning which seemed unas-
sailable. If there are no supernatural forces or spirits which could account
for mental phenomena, then the mind must be the brain and nothing
else." As a result of this or a similar mode of reasoning, phrenology
was adopted, championed, or seriously considered at various points not
only by Elliotson, who founded the Phrenological Society in 1824, but
also by Charles Bray, the author of *The Philosophy of Necessity* and a
friend of both George Combe, a dedicated phrenologist, and novelist
George Eliot, who had a phrenological cast made of her head. While
Charles Dickens set greater store by mesmerism, he too considered
phrenology, while Charlotte Brontë, who consented to a phrenological
examination, occasionally peppered her novels with allusions to phrenology and physiognomy that, according to Chase, provided among other
things "terse assessments of character." Phrenology, "less flamboyant,"
to borrow Oppenheim's words, than mesmerism, especially during the
early nineteenth century, certainly achieved a level of respectability not
vouchsafed kindred enthusiasms.[11]

Although the phrenologist, mesmerist, and spiritualist all aimed,
as Oppenheim puts it, to explain their "accomplishments in physical
terms," there remained a "nonmaterial strain." These fringe sciences
made the medical and scientific establishment uneasy, as it felt itself
visited by the specters of magic and supernaturalism from which it
was trying to free itself. "The subject of Animal Magnetism," wrote
distinguished nineteenth-century naturalist Alfred Russel Wallace, who

11. Chase, *Eros and Psyche,* 56; Oppenheim, *The Other World: Spiritualism and Psychical Research
in England, 1850–1914,* 211; Davies, *Phrenology: Fad and Science; a Nineteenth-Century American
Crusade,* 5; Purkis, *A Preface to George Eliot,* 34–36; Chase, *Eros and Psyche,* 54; Oppenheim, *The
Other World,* 210.

was both president of the Anthropological Society of London and a champion of spiritualism, "is still so much a disputed one among scientific men, and many of its alleged phenomena so closely border on, if they do not actually reach what is classed as supernatural, that I wish to give a few illustrations of the kind of facts by which it is supported." The business of doctors and scientists, men such as Michael Faraday, John Tyndall, and T. H. Huxley, would be ultimately to controvert these illustrations of the purported facts. "In the Victorian period," Oppenheim explains, "science and medicine were seeking to anchor themselves firmly in the physical world, distinctly divorced from all disreputable thought systems whose insubstantial foundations could cast doubt on the weightiness of the scientific endeavor. Mesmerism, spiritualism and even phrenology as well, had roots in a magical, occult past, where divination, humors, and conjured apparitions abounded." Like the figure of the ghost, the pseudosciences partook of two worlds, hovering somewhere between science and the supernatural, between the reality of the head and the mystery of the spirit.[12]

Interestingly enough, it was not only the pseudo but also the hard or legitimate sciences that opened a portal for the supernatural. Across the Atlantic, where spiritualism had got its start, literary man and advocate of spiritualism Epes Sargent wrote in *Planchette,* published in 1869,

> The further science carries its analysis, the more does the material world lose that character of rigidity which our external senses attach to it; and the more does it seem plastic under spiritual laws. Modern chemistry has shown us that all solid bodies may exist as aeriform; that even iron may be converted into an invisible gas; and the diamond which to our senses is inert, ponderable matter, may be volatilized in the fire of the burning mirror so as to develop neither smoke nor cinders. On the other hand, fire, essentially volatile, can be condensed in the calcination of metals, so as to become ponderable.

12. Oppenheim, *The Other World,* 210; Wallace, *Miracles and Modern Spiritualism,* 64 (for information about Wallace's part in the spiritualist movement and for an examination of how Wallace, a co-discoverer of natural selection, reconciled his scientific findings with his spiritualistic faith, see Oppenheim, *The Other World,* 297–325); Oppenheim, *The Other World,* 223. See also Fred Kaplan's *Dickens and Mesmerism: The Hidden Springs of Fiction,* in which he rightly notes the "utopian" aspects of mesmerism that "appealed to the heart as well as to the head," a mesmerism that "had not only a strand of scientific but also an elaborate weave of Romantic and revolutionary utopianism that contained threads from western society's inheritance of religion and magic" (7).

Science, then, according to Sargent and others such as De Montlosier, the French nobleman, statesman, and author of *Des Mystère de la vie humaine,* whom Sargent cites, was demonstrating how "all the bodies of the universe might be volatilized and made to disappear in those spaces which our ignorance calls *the void.*"[13] In other words, science gave palpable proof of how the solid or concrete could be transformed into the impalpable, the invisible, the ghostly. In this instance, chemistry created a twilight space that made the eerie phenomenal claims of the fringe sciences seem possible if not probable.

As much as the supernaturalism of mesmerism and spiritualism was the despair of science it was also the proverbial thorn in the episcopal side of the religious establishment, which found itself during the nineteenth century in some disarray. In a letter to her friend Ottilie von Goethe, art historian and social critic Anna Jameson in 1851 wrote that "between our Ultra-religionists, puseyites and non-believers we are in a charming state of confusion." In this condition, the church faced a powerful resurgence of supernaturalism. With its traditional and biblical ties to the otherworldly ideas of heaven and hell, of spirit possession and ghosts, the church ought logically to have had no difficulty with mesmerism, spiritualism, and ghosts. Certainly some spiritualists were quick to point out scripturally sanctioned precedents, and some members of the church as eagerly welcomed spiritualism. Thus, as late as 1900, one clergyman argued, "Indeed, Spiritualism fitted very nicely into Christianity. . . . In the first place, Spiritualism had rehabilitated the Bible." According to this clergyman, people "were asked to believe in Bible miracles, and at the same time taught that, outside the Bible records, nothing supernatural ever happened. But now the whole thing had been reversed. People now believed in the Bible because of Spiritualism; they did not believe in Spiritualism because of the Bible."[14] Despite the fact that mesmerism and spiritualism seemed to resurrect sacred miracles, the church did not necessarily or eagerly embrace either the new science or the new movement; on the whole, it was as distrustful of these phenomena as was science.

In his history of spiritualism, novelist Arthur Conan Doyle, who had a great interest in the subject, observed, "No class has shown itself so

13. *Planchette; or, The Despair of Science. Being a Full Account of Modern Spiritualism, Its Phenomena, and the Various Theories Regarding It. With a Survey of French Spiritism,* 374.
14. Jameson, "Letter 142"; Arthur Conan Doyle, *The History of Spiritualism,* 2:263.

sceptical and incredulous of modern Spiritual manifestations as those very clergy who profess complete belief in similar occurrences in bygone ages, and their utter refusal to accept them now is a measure of the sincerity of their professions." The church's refusal to recognize the phenomena of spiritualism was also a measure of ecclesiastical intimidation, for the religious establishment no doubt felt its authority threatened by the secularization and democratization of church affairs that occurred as both men and women began to claim more power over spiritual matters at the séance tables. As Howard Kerr, in his study of American spiritualism, observed, "The religious implication of this millennial impulse was that men no longer needed to depend on church and clergy and scripture for proof of the soul's immortality." While the church called for patience that would by and by net good Christians the Kingdom of God and a reunion with loved ones, séances where individuals could supposedly communicate through mediums with the dead offered more direct and immediately gratifying contact with the other side. The church stood on tradition, while spiritualism tried to stand on science: "Faith has been abused until it has become impossible to many earnest minds, and there is a call for proof and for knowledge. It is this which Spiritualism supplies. It founds our belief in life after death and in the existence of invisible worlds, not upon ancient tradition or upon vague intuitions, but upon proven facts, so that a science of religion may be built up, and man given a sure pathway amid the quagmire of the creeds."[15]

The resulting relations between scientific and ecclesiastical systems and supernaturalism were complex. Generally speaking, science had at some point undermined or refuted the claims of both the clergy and the supernaturalists. Yet clergymen who either denied the reality of spirits communicating with the living or denounced raps, taps, and spirits as demonology became by default the bedfellows of science, which would, one scholar has argued, supplant religion: "Science as it has become institutionalized has tended to make the same overriding claims as were previously made by religion, to be the 'Truth', and the only correct method of studying the universe. When science takes this step it changes from being an empirical study into a faith or 'religion'. . . . Science has

---

15. Doyle, *History of Spiritualism*, 2:248; Kerr, *Mediums, and Spirit-Rappers, and Roaring Radicals*, 11; Doyle, *History of Spiritualism*, 2:248.

become a faith for western man in the nineteenth and twentieth centuries." For those in the nineteenth century who were unsatisfied with the defunct supernaturalism of the church or with what William Johnston in 1851 called "the general faith in science as a wonder-worker," there was the vital supernaturalism of spiritualism. "An attempt to use scientific methods . . . to establish the existence of the supernatural,"[16] spiritualism sought to embrace both the religion and the science that repelled it.

Disavow it as they would, the priest, the scientist, the eminently practical man were all hard put to lay the supernatural to rest, especially because in England as well as in America spiritualism was "repeatedly bringing ghosts to public attention." Florence Marryat enthusiastically reported that she herself had converted hundreds of educated people, while William Howitt declared that spiritualism had "received the assent of about twenty millions of people in all countries." In 1881, Epes Sargent similarly maintained, "In less than forty years it [spiritualism] has gained at least twenty millions of adherents in all parts of the world. Adapting itself, through its eclectic affinity with all forms of truth, to all nationalities and classes, and repeating its peculiar manifestations everywhere."[17]

Exaggerated or not, these numbers attest to the significance of the ghosts that graced the séance tables. They figured so prominently in Victorian life that they got the attention of the illustrator and caricaturist George Cruikshank, whose business it was to identify and magnify issues endemic to his society. Intending to deliver a lighthearted but well-aimed blow to the pates of the spiritually gullible, Cruikshank in 1863 rapped the spirit-rappers:

> Now it will be as well here to inquire what good has ever resulted from this belief in what is commonly understood to be a ghost? None that I have ever heard of, and I have been familiar with all the popular ghost stories from boyhood, and have of late waded through almost all the works produced in support of this spiritual visiting theory, but in *no one instance* have I discovered where any beneficial result has followed from the supernatural or rather unnatural supposed appearances.

16. Geoffrey K. Nelson, *Spiritualism and Society*, 140; Johnston, *England as It Is: Political, Social, and Industrial in the Middle of the Nineteenth Century*, 1:245; Nelson, *Spiritualism and Society*, 140.

17. Kerr, *Mediums, and Spirit-Rappers, and Roaring Radicals*, 55; Howitt, "Letter," in *Report on Spiritualism*, 236; Sargent, *The Scientific Basis of Spiritualism*, 7.

Exasperated by all the concern about ghosts, the eminently practical Cruikshank responded with a question, "Wherein lies the utility of ghosts?" Having "waded" through a sea of "works produced in support of this spiritual visiting theory," Cruikshank could not discern the metaphorical or metaphysical charge spirits gave to corporeality, if not to corpses.[18]

According to Nina Auerbach, ghosts did offer certain "gifts" to Victorian men and women who sought to keep their faith from "disappear[ing] into the void of science." Having "nothing left to believe in but their lives," these men and women could "find spiritual authority in the revelations of a life" or a self, the "extraordinariness" of which was most intensely realized in death. "In the nineteenth-century imagination, death [that] gain[ed] stunning power," to vivify the self and to "crystallize . . . identities," would be realized in "the Victorian ghost, that spectacular epitome of the own self." Holding out "the vibrancy, the momentary transformations, the heightened, crystallized energy, of the stage," the ghost "embodi[ed] those intimations of potency the living dream of and fear." Ghosts concretized not just the afterlife but also being. Affirming as they did the staying power of life, ghosts figuratively if not literally filled the air of a people who both enjoyed the material prosperity that science and technology had brought about and yet reluctantly relinquished the idea of God or at least the transcendental feeling of "living on."[19]

The Victorians lived lives energized, perhaps sometimes enervated, by the contradiction inherent in this conflict. Nowhere did this energy, born of the complex relations among science, religion, and the supernatural, manifest itself more publicly, earnestly, or officially than in the establishment of the Psychical Society. Although the society was not the first of its kind, it was more widely recognized than its prototypes, for one thing because it, along with its sister branch in America, gathered, studied, and published the greatest wealth of material on occult phenomena.[20] The

18. George Cruikshank, *A Discovery Concerning Ghosts: With a Rap at the Spirit-Rappers,* 2

19. Auerbach, *Private Theatricals,* 107, 4, 3, 12, 89, 100, 93, 89, 107, 101. For an in-depth study of Victorians and death, see Garrett Stewart's *Death Sentences: Styles of Dying in British Fiction.* For recent critical and feminist explorations of death see Regina Barreca, ed., *Sex and Death in Victorian Literature;* Elisabeth Bronfen, *Over Her Dead Body: Death, Femininity, and the Aesthetic;* and Elisabeth Bronfen and Sarah Webster Goodwin, eds., *Death and Representation.* I borrow the expression *living on* from George Eliot's *The Lifted Veil,* 2.

20. See Oppenheim's section on "The Forerunners of the SPR" in *The Other World,* 123–35.

Society for Psychical Research may in fact be seen as an epistemological culmination of the Victorians' passion for assurances on the question of ghosts and thereby the meaning of life.

Victorians had in essence clamored for some resolution about the supernatural. No doubt, the failure of other agencies like the Dialectical Society to determine conclusively whether the supernatural was real, the remonstrances of such writers as Cruikshank, and the promptings of writers such as Catherine Crowe, who maintained "that whether these manifestations be from heaven or hell, or whether they exist at all or not, is a question that we have every right to ask of those who, having qualified themselves for investigations, are bound to answer"—these precipitated the birth of the society. For the question of ghosts proved so very pressing that the Victorians, led by a professor of physics, Sir William Barrett, finally organized on February 20, 1882, a learned society to employ rigorous scientific methods to settle, if possible, but certainly to investigate, the supernatural. In *Spiritualism and Nineteenth-Century Letters,* Russell and Clare Goldfarb give a role call of the Society for Psychical Research that impresses one with a sense of the age's ambivalent fascination with mystery and spirits and its commitment to science and factual inquiry:

> The Society for Psychical Research was founded by scientists and by spiritualists, by sons of clergymen and by graduates of Cambridge and Oxford; the founders were Barrett, Henry Sidgwick, the first president of the Society, Frederic W. H. Myers, Edmund Gurney, and Frank Podmore, a civil servant among academics and natural philosophers; the spiritualist members were the Reverend W. Stainton Moses, Morell Theobald, Dr. George Wild, and Dawson Rogers. A distinguished physicist, Oliver Lodge, joined the group in the 1890s, but by this time the Society had a number of eminent members: W. E. Gladstone and Arthur Balfour, Prime Ministers; eight Fellows of the Royal Society, including Alfred Russel Wallace, Lord Rayleigh, and Balfour Stewart; the poet laureate of England, Alfred Tennyson; and other literary figures such as John Ruskin, "Lewis Carroll," and John Addington Symonds. Nearly one thousand people joined the Society for Psychical Research in its first decade of existence.

That only women are missing from this list of the founding assembly, which constituted a mix of skeptics, believers, and the undecided, of those from academic, scientific, political, and religious communities, is

indicative of Victorian determination to get at the heart of the supernatural fuss by pooling as many male perspectives as possible.[21]

While "psychical researchers were interested in all types of inexplicable phenomena," those that called the question most insistently were
ghosts.[22] "We may defy the supporters of this apparition doctrine to
bring forward one circumstance in connection with these ghosts, which
corresponds in any way with the real character of the CREATOR, where
any real benefit has been known to result from such sounds and such
appearances—none, none, none," Cruikshank insisted, then continued,

> whereas we know that there has been a large amount of human suf-
> fering, illness, folly, and mischief, and in former times, we know, to a
> large and serious extent, but even now, in this "age of intellect," when
> we come to investigate the causes of some of the most painful diseases
> amongst children and young persons, particularly young females, we
> find, on the authority of the first medical men, that they are occasioned
> by being frightened by mischievous, thoughtless, or cruel persons,
> mainly in consequence of being *taught in their childhood to believe
> in ghosts.*[23]

The fact of the matter is that although Cruikshank and other skeptics
like Huxley, who finally equated the folly of spiritual manifestations
with the twaddle of curates and women, would have liked very much to
relegate ghosts to the domains of old women's chatter, children's boogie
bears, and young girls' prepubescent anxiety, spirits there were abroad
in Victorian England, which found itself in the anomalous position of
being the most haunted age of intellect.

21. Crowe, *Spiritualism and the Age We Live In*, 141; Goldfarb and Goldfarb, *Spiritualism and Nineteenth-Century Letters*, 128. In all fairness, women would become a part of the Society, which eventually had a woman president in Eleanor Balfour Sidgwick.
22. Mary Walker, "Between Fiction and Madness: The Relationship of Women to the Supernatural in Late Victorian Britain," 231.
23. Cruikshank, *A Discovery*, 20.

2

A SPIRIT OF HER OWN
NINETEENTH-CENTURY FEMININE
EXPLORATIONS OF SPIRITUALITY

*W*HILE VICTORIAN scientists, doctors, lawyers, manufacturers, and even clergymen sought "to anchor themselves firmly in the physical" as well as the rational and material world, wives, mothers, daughters, and sisters were being positioned elsewhere. In "Victorian Science and the 'Genius' of Woman," Flavia Alaya examines how science called into question, if indeed it did not mount an attack on, woman's intellectual and artistic capacities and abilities: "Gallantry was being swept away by dogmatic scientific conclusiveness, in assertions that not only described the observable range of women's collective 'genius' but defined—and often prescribed—the upward limits of its exercise in the individual, i.e., the capacity of women for any exceptional achievement." More recently, Elizabeth K. Helsinger, Robin Lauterbach Sheets, and William Veeder, in *The Woman Question,* shed further light on this scientific disabling of women: "Most scientists and physicians throughout the Victorian period define woman's sphere narrowly. This puts science in an awkward position; the prestige of scientific arguments derives partly from their supposed 'objectivity,' and yet the scientific arguments about women are anything but unbiased. Recent historians have documented conclusively how Victorian science handpicked and egregiously bent

27

facts to support foregone conclusions." Darwin's discovery of evolution by natural selection would allow some members of the scientific establishment to buttress traditional beliefs about woman's lower ranking on "a hieratic scale of increasing perfection."[1] Thus the Spencerians (named after Herbert Spencer), who "gained much prestige by popular association with *The Origin of Species,*" concluded that since "evolution proceeds towards increased specialization" woman would "become ever more maternal as man becomes ever more intelligent."[2] The efforts of the legitimate sciences were clearly to keep women, much as they kept the pseudosciences in which women would play an important role, peripheral—or, more accurately, somewhere between the margin and the center.

Thus, while science placed women, as Cynthia Eagle Russett indicates in *Sexual Science,* somewhere between man and ape, Victorian society at large found it socially, morally, and culturally beneficial to locate woman between man and angel as a handmaid to "that male genius . . . synonymous with British civilization, which depended heavily on the establishment of the empire of science." In fact, the Victorians may be said to have reinvested their beleaguered spirituality in those culturally pedastaled but biologically and intellectually limited vessels, their women. By doing so Victorians were after all reaffirming a primitive, age-old connection between mystery and women, whose powers—"bleeding painlessly in rhythm with the moon, drawing *people* from their bodies, producing food from their bodies for the young"[3]—had inspired in early men both fear and awe.

By the Victorian period the patriarchy had qualified and contained these powers by socially and culturally reconstructing them. Childbearing and especially menstruation were seen in the masculine world as debilities: they were traditionally associated with weakness, uncleanliness, and hysteria. As Charlene Spretnak in her introduction to *The*

---

1. Alaya, "Victorian Science and the 'Genius' of Woman," 264; Helsinger, Sheets, and Veeder, *The Woman Question: Society and Literature in Britain and American, 1837–1883,* 2:56, 89.

2. Michael Shortland, "Spencer, Herbert," in Sally Mitchell, ed., *Victorian Britain: An Encyclopedia,* 746; Helsinger, Sheets, and Veeder, *The Woman Question,* 90.

3. In *Sexual Science: The Victorian Construction of Womanhood,* Russett argues, "Women and the lesser races served to buffer Victorian gentlemen from a too-threatening intimacy with the brutes" (14). Alaya, "Victorian Science," 268; Charlene Spretnak, introduction to Spretnak, ed., *The Politics of Women's Spirituality,* xii.

Politics of Women's Spirituality notes, "Since men could never possess the elemental power that women have, they sought to hoard all the cultural, i.e., invented, power. Toward this end, they created ludicrous myths that belie the truths of nature, e.g., Zeus giving birth to His daughter Athena by having Her spring from His forehead (fully armed and ready to defend Daddy's property!), and Yahweh/God the Father birthing the Earth and all its creatures by performing some tricky sleights of hand." Enhancing patriarchal power meant casting female power in a different light because, Spretnak continues, "Patriarchal culture also denigrated the formerly sacred menstrual blood and childbirth, declaring that both render women categorically 'unclean.'" In *The Trial of Woman*, a study of the relationship of the women's movement in England to the "woman question," science, and the occult, one of Diana Basham's most provocative and central recognitions is that the "female menstrual cycle [was] itself a site for anxious discussion about the legendary occult powers of 'Woman.'" The issue of menstruation, asserts Basham, "appears as both crucial and occult, simultaneously central and unmentionable. [Although] menstruation was a topic that was seldom addressed directly . . . it was a key concept because of all that it implied concerning women's biological and psychic 'difference.'" Yet from woman's difference, from her body, came the miracle of children, heirs to property and the family name. In the Victorian period, as in no other hitherto, the "elemental power" of woman's body was being both played up to keep her in the home and played down or at least overridden to emphasize a potent but apparently less threatening spiritual facility. Acclaimed, after the ideal woman in Coventry Patmore's poem, as "The Angel in the House," woman was granted the power "to soften and attract," to be a gentle moral force in the home. So long as she ministered to the comfort of her husband, tended the children, managed the household, all was well. However, when she began to assert herself beyond the domestic realm, her special powers became equivocal. At best her ultradomestic energies were hysterical; at worst these energies were seen, Nina Auerbach argues, as demonic.[4]

4. Spretnak, introduction to *The Politics of Women's Spirituality*, xiii; Basham, *Trial of Woman*, vii; see Coventry Patmore's *The Angel in the House*. I have borrowed the phrase, "to soften and attract" from Mary Shelley's *Frankenstein, or the Modern Prometheus*, 38; see Auerbach's *The Woman and the Demon*.

Ultimately, one of the effects of science's efforts to shake free of the supernatural was the shifting of specters and such into the realm of the feminine and the weak where old men in their dotage talk of miracles; where women chatter themselves into something resembling hysteria; where children, corrupted, according to the father of rationalism John Locke, by that lower order of beings the servants, fear things that go bump in the night. The female is specterized; women become associated with the numinous and the natural in a peculiar kind of supernatural-ization that reroutes emphasis from the physical feat of woman's child-bearing to the more sacralized social function of mothering, which in turn renders woman's intellectual and material contributions to society less solid. What this kind of redefinition creates is an even stronger metaphorical link between women and supernaturalism. It was women who, after all, had the truly haunted intellects, whose "collective genius" was suspended between their maternal powers and their limited intellec-tual achievement. Inasmuch as they found themselves and their powers equivocalized, hystericized, and spiritualized, Victorian women were at some more profound level the real ghosts in the Victorian noontide.

One of the ways in which nineteenth-century British women them-selves addressed, manifested, and explored the spirituality their age granted them and the specterhood shifted onto them was through writing about and participating in such supernatural phenomena as mes-merism and spiritualism. The ascendancy of heart, soul, and sympathy in the feminine sex, whether indeed innate or merely culturally ingrained, seemed to make women the ideal disseminators of spiritual beliefs and experiences. In *Woman in the Nineteenth Century,* Margaret Fuller credits the nineteenth-century woman with an "especial genius" that is "electrical in movement, intuitive in function, spiritual in tendency," an ability to seize causes instinctively, and a talent for the "simple breathing out of what she receives, that has the singleness of life, rather than the selecting and energizing of art." Elsewhere, Fuller emphasizes the special spiritual nature of the female, remarking that the great Italian poets "saw that, in cases where the right direction had been taken, the greater delicacy of her [the lover/woman's] frame and stillness of her life left her more open than is Man to spiritual influx."[5]

5. Fuller, *Woman in the Nineteenth Century, and Kindred Papers Relating to the Sphere, Condition, and Duties of Woman,* 115, 69.

Equally, if not more, attuned to the distinct spirituality of the female, Catherine Crowe in *The Night Side of Nature* explains:

> The circumstance, too, that phenomena of this kind [dreams, pre-
> sentiments, ghost-seeing] are more frequently developed in women
> than in men, and that they are merely the consequence of her greater
> nervous irritability has been made another objection to them—an
> objection, however, which Dr. Passavant [German physician and writer
> Johann Karl Passavant] considers founded on ignorance of the essential
> difference between the sexes, which is not merely a physical but a
> psychological one. Man is more productive than receptive. . . .
>
> Thus the extatic [*sic*] woman will be more frequently a seer, in-
> stinctive and intuitive; man, a doer and a worker; and as all genius is
> a degree of extacy or clear-seeing, we perceive the reason wherefore in
> man it is more productive than in woman.

Crowe, a pioneer in the field of parapsychology, apparently felt no qualms in noting the distinctions between the spiritually receptive female and the materially productive male. "It is alleged, then," she wrote elsewhere, "that these phenomena never appear spontaneously, or can be evoked, except in persons more or less diseased, or in weak women and impressionable children. . . . But what of that?" Women who more easily entered into mesmerism and spiritualism were regarded as being more open to "higher truths" than men; they were hailed for being more open to spiritual knowledge.[6] The angel in the house could be a powerful conduit for the spirituality, the mystery, and the supernaturalism that the age craved but science discredited.

As evidence of the legitimacy of the supernatural and further documentation of woman's special role and powers, Crowe translated Justinus Kerner's *Die Seherin von Prevorst*. The German doctor Kerner had kept the seer Frederica Hauffe under close surveillance, at one point moving her into his own home. He witnessed the mesmeric trances during which the seer conversed with her guardian spirit, the efficacy of the cures she, while deep in mesmeric sleep, prescribed for ailing neighbors who sought her medical advice, and her preternatural powers of prevision and vision. On occasion, in experimenting with her powers, he noted that the "nipples of a horse, the tooth of a mammoth, bezoar, a spider's

6. Crowe, *The Night Side of Nature; or, Ghosts and Ghost Seers*, 1:383–84, and *Spiritualism and the Age We Live In*, 91, 13.

web, a glow-worm, &c. &c., all produced specific effects on being placed in her hand." Other experiments he conducted on the seer centered on water, gravity, "imponderable substances," the human eye, and the pit of the stomach, among other areas. Through Frederica Hauffe, Kerner became more convinced that "there is a super-terrestrial world."[7]

With her clairvoyant powers and her inner hot line to the dead, the simple, sensitive, mountain-bred Frederica Hauffe amazed and impressed Doctor Kerner. But what apparently most amazed and troubled even this open-minded medical observer was the seer's sex. "It is certainly hard," complained Kerner, "and we cannot wonder at the annoyance it occasions, that a weak silly woman should thus disturb the established systems of the learned, and revive persuasions that it has long been the aim of the wise among men to eradicate." But Kerner availed himself of a biblical touchstone for reassurance, Paul's first Epistle to the Corinthians (1:27, 26): "But God hath chosen the foolish things of the world to confound the wise; and God hath chosen the weak things of the world to confound the things which are mighty."[8]

While Kerner bemoaned the fact that "a weak silly woman" should challenge "the established systems of the . . . wise among men," Crowe, whose translation of *Die Seherin* helped to make the seer a legend among spiritualists, elsewhere offered a scientific explanation for the faculties of the clairvoyant female: "it is doubtless, from the greater development of the ganglionic system in women, that they exhibit more frequent instances of such abnormal phenomena [presentiments, dreams, ghost-seeing, etc.] as I am treating of, than men."[9]

At least one of Britain's leading medical journals, the *Lancet,* was skeptical of mesmerism and the seers who practiced it. Launching an attack on mesmerism, the *Lancet* singled out the spiritual proclivity of females as an aberration:

> All the malingering of the age has a natural determination towards mesmerism. Of such imposters the sisters OKEY may be considered the type. In some cases there is no actual deceit, but merely a morbid

7. Kerner, *The Seeress of Prevorst, Being Revelations Concerning the Inner-Life of Man, and the Interfusion of a World of Spirits in the One We Inhabit,* 68, 71, 151.
8. Ibid., 4.
9. Crowe, *Night Side,* 1:104–5.

desire to parade these disorders, real or imaginary, before the public eye; or they deceive themselves, and really believe in the existence of diseases and the occurrence of cures. Affected by a depraved appetite, like that which impels certain descriptions of patients to eat the dirt of the most loathsome corners . . . so these semi-patients and semi-dupes, affected by a moral pica, delight to dwell upon disgusting or indelicate details. . . . In this way the celebrated authoress of the preventive check parades her diseased vagina and os uteri as it were in a public speculum before the general gaze, and other ladies write and publish pamphlets about their uterine symptoms and their disorders of sex, in a manner to have made our grandmothers sink into the earth for shame. The sensations, disorders, credulity, cunning, and self-deceptions of this class of subjects, and the simplicity of the great number who credulously believe in them, form the other great division of the mesmeric array.[10]

The attack on mesmerism becomes an ad hominem attack on women. The *Lancet* article pointedly fails to mention any male dupes; instead, it centers its vituperative assault on women, depicting them as "diseased" and feeble-willed trash receptacles rather than as receptive human beings. These presumably hysterical women were, the journal suggests, the gulls and "semi-dupes" of abominable, bogus fads like mesmerism and spiritualism not only because of their psychologically "morbid desires" and "depraved appetites" but also because of the very things that made them female: the "vagina" and "os uteri."

As the *Lancet* article suggests, some Victorian males became highly uneasy about such female modes of escape as mesmerism and spiritualism. While female practitioners of these weird phenomena initially seemed to be minding their own ethereal business and leaving worldly affairs to men, they were nonetheless threatening to subvert the patriarchally designated Christian roles of the quiet, obedient, homebound angel or to extend those roles in such a way as to criticize masculine hegemony. Thus, Marie Sinclair, Countess of Caithness, who claimed to have a spiritual connection with Mary Stuart, found that the spiritual teachings of the supernaturalized female could and ought to offset, if not challenge, men's materialism. "Men," the spirit of Mary Stuart is said to have warned the countess, "are asleep over the material triumphs they

10. "Mesmeric Deceptions—The Whipton Prophetess"; the "celebrated authoress" may refer to Harriet Martineau, who did suffer menstrual problems.

are crowning their brows with, or so buried amid the burdens of life, they cannot be still and listen to the voice of Deific forces. But Woman [*sic*], the earth's Mothers, must do so—must be earnest and active, or her feet will sink into the mire of revolutionary forces. Material burial is the fate of all who are not every whit whole, who cannot bring new bodies into the heavenly kingdom."[11]

The exhibitionism the *Lancet* writer derides may be exaggerated, but it is undeniably true that things spiritual afforded Victorian women an outlet for self-assertion as well as notoriety, attention, and a means of capitalizing on the intuitive powers with which they were credited by a society that regarded them otherwise as intellectually barren. The writer Charlotte Yonge, who, as Katharine Moore notes, was a firm believer in the "subjection of women," nonetheless insisted that such subjection by no means extended to spiritual matters: "Women are not only allowed but encouraged to call their *souls* their own and so they retain their dignity in spite of all the meek obedience demanded of them." The very supernatural that could leave women open to charges of irrationality and sexual dysfunction could also provide them with new contexts for speech and action, a freed voice for their conscious and unconscious feelings, a higher regard for their persons and for their neglected minds. What women want, wrote Margaret Fuller, is "the freedom, the religious, the intelligent freedom of the universe to use its means, to learn its secret, as far as Nature has enabled them, with God alone for their guide and their judge." The debate over the legitimacy of mesmerism and spiritualism, indeed even of ghosts, would afford women the opportunity not only to publicize their personal experiences and beliefs in the weird phenomena and, in some instances, to investigate the role of the church, but also to enlist, consciously and unconsciously, the attention of a popular audience as well as a professional and scientific one. It was not just the "death and magic" Regina Barreca identifies but also, especially for the Victorians, I contend, the pseudosciences and ghosts that could become "the effective tools of those considered ineffective."[12]

Interestingly enough, Harriet Martineau, a noted rationalist and writer on religion, economy, and government, vehemently decried any

11. Marie Sinclair, Countess of Caithness, *A Midnight Visit to Holyrood*, 38.
12. Moore, *Victorian Wives*, 150; Fuller, *Woman in the Nineteenth Century*, 63; Barreca, "Writing as Voodoo: Sorcery, Hysteria, and Art," 177.

form of supernatural hocus-pocus, though she staunchly credited the mesmerism the *Lancet* denounced. Disparaging the mysteries of providence and supernaturalism as figments of a mind slipped back into black and obscure error, Martineau wondered, "How many entire ghosts have thus presented themselves from the mere fragments of resemblance to the human form! How many gleams of moonlight, how many nodding twigs, how many scudding clouds have inspired needless terror!" One road that might lead from the dusty darkness of unreality to empirically substantial reality was, as Martineau suggested, to be found in nature:

> And what a *feeling* it is,—that which grows up and pervades us when we have fairly returned to our obedience to Nature! What a healthful glow animates the faculties! . . . One seems to have even a new set of nerves, when one has planted one's foot on the broad common of Nature, and clear daylight, and bracing breezes are about one, and there are no more pitfalls and rolling vapors,—no more raptures and agonies of selfish hope and fear,—but sober certainty of reliance on the immutability of Nature's laws.

With her Wordsworthian love of nature, and her eighteenth-century Lockean belief in the senses and reason, Harriet Martineau could decide that "the philosopher is safe in his conclusion that as the material frame cannot be renovated, and as the spiritual one is not recognisable by the senses, the dead do not appear to the living." Instead ghosts, deities, and other such superstitious folly, the agnostic Martineau insisted, were often the work of a "few individuals who, by skill or accident, had anticipated scientific facts now generally known, [and] turned their knowledge to profitable account by imposing on the imaginations of the ignorant many."[13]

Martineau not only attacked the supernatural that thinkers such as Crowe and later Sophia De Morgan sought to "palliate" with science and reason, she also attacked religious supernaturalism and its proponents. The clergy, as Martineau saw it, also had a hand in nursing supernaturalism: "We still find the devil the bugbear, and the clergy the managers. We still find that the ignorant are cajoled, and that orthodoxy is propped

13. Martineau, "Demonology and Witchcraft," in *Miscellanies*, 2:98–99; Martineau and Henry George Atkinson, *Letters on the Laws of Man's Nature and Development*, 290; Martineau, "Demonology and Witchcraft," in *Miscellanies*, 2:95, 96.

up by the false supports of superstition." As an appendix to her *Society in America*, Martineau included an excerpt from an 1833 publication, *Aladdin's Lamp*, in which clergymen are accused of taking particularly shameless advantage of women who

> in all matters relating to religion . . . naturally reverence and cling to those who show them respect and deference. The clergy, from understanding this point in their nature, possess great and deserved influence over them; and they have only to interest their feelings, to insure success to any clerical or charitable purpose. . . . And will she not toil for days, scarcely raising her eyes from the work, to assist in purchasing an organ, a new altar-cloth, or in cleaning and painting a church?
>
> So great is the tax, now, on a woman's time, for these and for other religious purposes, such as the "educating young men for the ministry," that the amount is frightful and scandalous.

Such exploitation of women in the name of God, as well as the supernaturalism of charlatans and clergymen, could not be disposed of until "every man ascertains and applies his Christianity for himself" and until people come to "expose indefatigably the machinery of spiritual delusion; to frown upon all spiritual monopoly; to reveal to the ignorant their own rights, and to protect their claim."[14]

For the philosophical, agnostic Martineau, the only apparitions that plagued mankind were those projected by imposture or by a malfunctioning nervous system or overheated brain. "Apparitions, then," she determined, "are seen when ideas are so vivified as to overpower actual impressions," and this vivification of ideas often results from illness or mental excitement.[15] She was sympathetic to the idea that people in bereavement, affected by illness, or merely eager to enrich daily existence imaginatively could yearn for such things as ghosts, but that they should actually believe these superstitions was more than any sensible person could countenance.

Yet the hardheaded, rationalist, and professionally reputable Martineau, who explicitly attacked supernaturalism, gave hearty credence to mesmerism, that shady phenomenon with decided supernatural overtones. Admittedly, she saw nothing supernatural in mesmerism, but then

14. Martineau, "On Witchcraft," in *Miscellanies*, 2:402; appendix to *Society in America*, 415; "On Witchcraft," in *Miscellanies*, 2:402.

15. Martineau, "Demonology and Witchcraft," in *Miscellanies*, 2:109, 112.

neither did Charles Dickens and Dr. John Elliotson of the University of London, who both practiced it. She set all the theories proposed to explain the phenomenon at naught and was, in spite of her philosophical turn of mind, quite content for the time being simply to relish its effectiveness without actually knowing its origin and cause. In the final analysis, she supposed this miraculous phenomenon to be one of the natural but heretofore uncultivated powers of humankind and, having thus explained away what smacked of the supernatural, proceeded herself to mesmerize some of her sick neighbors in the Lake District. Still, this phenomenon that Martineau so gratefully credited in her *Letters on Mesmerism* was the very same that the previously cited *Lancet* article attacked, only two years later, as the "professed science" of hysterical women, a bogus, and an "infamy."[16]

Despite such attacks on the phenomenon by fellow skeptics, Martineau remained firmly anchored in the ranks of the credulous. "My recovery now," she proclaimed, "by means of mesmeric treatment alone, has given me the most thorough knowledge possible that Mesmerism is true." The horrible internal disease that had imprisoned her in a room for five years was cured in miraculous mesmeric sessions to which she attributed a supernatural aura quite similar to that "machinery of illusion" she had so vehemently denounced in others:

> Twenty minutes from the beginning of the *séance*, I became sensible of an extraordinary appearance, most unexpected, and wholly unlike anything I had ever conceived of. Something seemed to diffuse itself through the atmosphere . . . most like a clear twilight, closing in from the windows and down from the ceiling, and in which one object after another melted away, till scarcely anything was visible before my wide-open eyes . . . then . . . the busts re-appeared, ghost-like.[17]

The rationalist who had earlier praised the "clear daylight" now found herself in "a clear twilight." Obviously, Martineau did not feel the disgust for mesmerism that another great agnostic writer, George Eliot, would later feel. If anything, Martineau's mesmeric experience gave her

16. See Martineau's *Miss Martineau's Letters on Mesmerism*, 22, on the explanations for mesmerism; "Mesmeric Deceptions—The Whipton Prophetess," 178.

17. Martineau, *Letters on Mesmerism*, 4, 5. See also Basham's discussion of how the mesmeric cure of Martineau's menstrual disorder paved the way for a "guilt-free use of . . . talents and capabilities" (*Trial of Woman*, 78).

a sympathetic understanding of how mesmerism could be interpreted supernaturally.

Perhaps Martineau, who coauthored with Henry George Atkinson what Charlotte Brontë described as "the first exposition of avowed Atheism and Materialism I have ever read; the first unequivocal declaration of disbelief in the existence of a God or a Future Life I have ever seen"— perhaps Martineau discovered in mesmerism a phenomenon that allowed her to come as close as she ever could to a type of religious ecstasy she could enjoy and sanction intellectually. She was clearly thrilled by more than a release from pain; the new sense she had discovered helped her to compensate for her impaired ones. Mesmerism revealed a new faculty that would enable her to apprehend more of the nature around her, and it opened up new vistas of that freedom and knowledge she had always valued: "Ignorant as we yet are,—hardly able yet . . . to snatch a glimpse of the workings of Nature . . . obvious as it is that our condition is merely that of infant-waking upon the world of existence, the privilege of freedom, as far as we are able to go, is quite inestimable." Finally, with its promise of a communication achieved without the use of the ordinary senses, mesmerism must have also afforded her a psychologically gratifying communion with fellow creatures from whom she must inevitably have felt cut off by the handicap of her deafness. Probably the most eminent member of that numerous class of Victorian women to whom mesmerism appealed, the professional invalid, Martineau nonetheless defies the easy stereotyping of the *Lancet*.[18] Whatever the reasons for her belief in mesmerism, Martineau was hardly a hysteric. Yet this unique and skeptical woman was far closer than she realized, or would have liked, to many a naive believer in the supernatural.

Whereas Martineau put her faith in a verifiable "daylight" of nature and natural causes, Crowe believed that the phenomena labeled supernatural were glimpses of a side of nature usually hidden from view. Crowe, who never claimed personally to have experienced the efficacy of

---

18. Clement Shorter, *The Brontës: Life and Letters, Being an Attempt to Present a Full and Final Record of the Lives of the Three Sisters* . . . , 2:197; Martineau and Atkinson, *Man's Nature and Development,* 290; for more information on the professional invalid and the appeal of mesmerism see Pearsall, *The Table-Rappers,* 24. See also Diana Basham's more recent and specific account of Martineau's impatience with the "mystical enthusiasms" of another well-known Victorian invalid, Elizabeth Barrett Browning, who had at one point been convinced of the claims of spiritualism (*Trial of Woman,* 79).

mesmerism or to have seen a ghost, had, nevertheless, witnessed strange phenomena. She had seen "tables move without any hand touching them" and "candles extinguished" unaccountably. She had also "held a guitar" while "chords were struck" mysteriously. "Being desired by the invisible Intelligence to sing," she wrote, "I was regularly accompanied through several songs."[19] On October 15, 1858, Crowe declined to say publicly whether she had ever seen a ghost.[20] About halfway into her *Ghosts and Family Legends,* she did, however, give an account of her visit to a haunted house. Although she saw no ghosts herself, by holding the hand of a clairvoyant young female, Crowe perceived strange "waves of white light." Of this honestly stated but rather anticlimactic jaunt to a haunted house, Crowe comments at length:

> You see our results were not great, but the visit was not wholly barren to me. Of course, many wise people will say, I did not see the lights, but that they were the offspring of my excited imagination. But I beg to say that my imagination was by no means excited. If I had been there *alone,* it would have been a different affair; for though I never saw a ghost nor ever fancied I did, I am afraid I should have been very nervous. But I was in exceedingly good company, with two very clever men, besides the lawyer, a lady, and the clairvoyante; so that my nerves were perfectly composed, as I should not object to seeing any ghost in such agreeable society. Moreover, I did not *expect* any result; because, there is very seldom any on these occasions, as ghosts appear we know not why; but certainly not because people wish to see them. They generally come when least expected and least thought of.[21]

Crowe's candor, her truthful and understated account of the particulars of her visit to the haunted house, reminds one of Martineau's equally factual defense of mesmerism. By discounting the idea of female hysteria or an "excited imagination" and by engaging the notable company of "two very clever men, besides a lawyer," as well as two other persons, Crowe seeks to validate the significance of "results" that others—lawyers, doctors, and priests—would be disposed to set aside.

Clearly nothing of a spiritual nature could be "wholly barren" to someone like Crowe, who devoted so much time and effort to championing supernaturalism in the face of disbelief, materialism, and "persons

---

19. Crowe, *Spiritualism and the Age We Live In,* 106–7.
20. Crowe, *Ghosts and Family Legends: A Volume for Christmas,* vii.
21. Ibid., 140, 142.

in authority, in this case, being the scientific world." Crowe herself became an authority on what is called the supernatural. Although her efforts on behalf of the nightside would be compromised, as Basham observes, by her nervous breakdown, Crowe's work was indeed "painstaking" and "pioneering." Her *Night Side of Nature*, which covers every form of spiritual manifestation from dreams to ghosts, is a Victorian bible of supernaturalism. In her preface, Crowe, who notes that science in England had "put it [the supernatural] aside as beneath her notice," is careful to relate her undertaking to the writings of German authors including Henrick Schubert, who produced, in Crowe's words, "a sort of cosmogony of the world, written in a spirit of philosophical mysticism— too much so for English readers." Denying the "pretension of *teaching* or of enforcing opinions," Crowe seeks "to suggest enquiry and stimulate observation" and to "induce a few capable persons, instead of laughing at these things, to look at them."[22]

Although she never claimed to be a spiritualist, eleven years after the publication of *Night Side*, Crowe, at the request of her English and American friends, became one of the first to write on "the vexed question of Spiritualism." In her *Spiritualism and the Age We Live In*, Crowe not only argues characteristically for open-mindedness on this topic but also, like Martineau, takes the opportunity to criticize dogmatic religion, which was fast becoming dry, worldly, and ineffective.

> Nor can we wonder at the small moral influence of dogmatic religion, and the inefficiency of these promises and threats to make men virtuous, when they cannot fail to observe how little their pastors themselves are affected by them. Ambition, love of dominion, too eager desire for wealth and worldly advantages, jealousy, intolerance, are the characteristics of all churches; insomuch, that it is the constant care of wise governments to avoid throwing too much power into their hands. That church that has the most, makes the worst use of it; priests, of whatever denomination, are no better than other men; and religion is, in fact, rather an engine of government, and a reinforcement to the police, than a saving health to men's souls.

Spiritualism seemed an invitingly viable alternative to the "empty formalism" of dogmatism. While it corresponded to the "rapid advance

---

22. Crowe, *Spiritualism and the Age We Live In*, 105; Basham, *Trial of Woman*, 153–54; Crowe, *Night Side*, 1:vi–viii.

of physical science," it also had a "tendency to generate or revivify the essentials of Religion, which are the emotions of the soul and its consciousness of immediate intercourse with God." As Mary Howitt, who coedited with her husband a history of the supernatural, would also note, what she initially thought a delusion had "in many cases . . . produced such beautiful and sincere religious faith and trust." Spiritualism, which was based on communication with the dead through a medium, purportedly by means of some electrical field, seemed what a religion should be—"an emotion arising out of knowledge, not a form founded on prescription."[23]

One writer who actually adopted and defended spiritualism as a religion was Florence Marryat, the daughter of author and naval officer Captain Frederic Marryat. Calling, as Crowe had earlier, for open-mindedness as well as for the right of people to decide for themselves, Marryat soon declared how she herself had decided:

> Let us resolve to know everything, and judge for ourselves! If we find Spiritualism does us harm, prevents our doing our duty in this world, or saps our health and strength, by all means abandon its pursuit, for it is not for us. But if it gives us comfort and pleasure, more faith in the goodness of God, and courage to do the work He has appointed us on earth, then cling to it as the greatest solace He has allotted Man. . . . *I* believe it to be an unmitigated blessing.

For Marryat, the "unmitigated blessing" of spiritualism was "a subject which is a religion to me." In her spiritualistic manifesto, *The Spirit World*, Marryat wrote, "If Spiritualism is wrong, God is wrong, and the Christ is wrong, and the Bible is wrong, and you have nothing left to cling to for time or eternity." While spiritualism thus incorporates elements of orthodox religion, there nonetheless remains a recognized antagonism between the two:

> The dead are *not* dead! They stand in our midst to-day. I, who write for you, have seen them, conversed with them, and handled them; and I would not part with the knowledge thus gained for all the good this world could give me. I allow that, in these days, it is not a common

23. Crowe, *Spiritualism and the Age We Live In*, [iii], 23, 48, 54; Howitt, *Mary Howitt, an Autobiography*, 2:105; Crowe, *Spiritualism and the Age We Live In*, 54.

experience. Would that it were! For centuries Spiritualism has been banned by the Church and thrust out of sight as an unclean thing. The Church, which encourages the State in upholding laws which are totally opposed to the teaching of its professed master Christ; which solemnises marriages which are nothing less than prostitution; which permits divorce, capital punishment, actions at law, winks at simony, and allots enormous revenues to its bishops and arch-bishops, whilst the poor rot and starve—this same Church forbids us to have any communication with spirits, who are the very first to denounce its corrupt practices.[24]

According to Marryat, established religion affords no comfort to the harried classes of people, among whom women are numbered, but rather encourages or condones the state in oppressing these people.

Fervent as Marryat was in her convictions about spiritualism, she was not so sentimental or irrational as to overlook the need for organization and revenue in the spiritual cause:

I contend that the Spiritualist should no more expect to enjoy the privileges of *his* religion for nothing than the Christian. We live in an age of greed and heavy expenses. Nothing is to be had for nothing in the year of our Lord 1894, and the time is past when congregations could assemble under the green-wood tree to hold their meetings of prayer and praise. A Spiritualist Society must have a room to assemble in, and preachers to conduct its services, just like the Christians, and such luxuries have to be paid for. . . . And why should mediums, who expend far more strength on the exercise of their profession than any of the clergy, be grudged the reward due to their great work?[25]

The Spiritualist Society that Marryat proposed would create a new profession—that of the medium—and thereby open up new social and religious horizons.

Marryat herself claimed modest powers as a medium: "I am a physical medium, and though I cannot procure materialisations by myself, I am said to impart much force to those I sit with." Her argumentative and persuasive powers in *There Is No Death* and *The Spirit World* proved even more formidable, it would seem, than her mediumistic powers. Helen Black, a contemporary of Florence Marryat's, reported that Marryat "numbers her converts [to Spiritualism] by the hundred and they are

24. Marryat, *The Spirit World*, 26, 8, 39, 38.
25. Ibid., 286–87.

all gathered from educated people; men of letters and of science have written to her from every part of the world, and many clergymen have succumbed to her courageous assertions."[26]

Spiritualism was just one of the means through which Victorian women could present their profoundly ambivalent responses to Christianity. For while Christianity, as Martineau shrewdly pointed out, filled the vacuity in some women's lives, and while some women saw in Christianity a release from the narrowness of their roles, others felt that Christianity, with its emphasis on obedience and self-sacrifice, reinforced the limiting role of angel in the house.[27] As we have seen, Crowe recognized it as an "engine of government"; later, Marryat would see it as the tool of a paternalistic state.

Yet it was science that remained the prime antagonist. Uncomfortable with the notion of instinct and spirit, scientists, according to Crowe, were limiting their knowledge. "Reason," she argues, "is a very valuable endowment certainly; but till it can teach us the way to truth, it is quite evident that, either we do not know how to use it, or that it is not so supreme a gift as the despised gift of instinct." An excessive reliance on reason, according to Crowe, could only lead to the materialism that she despised. "At a period when life has grown into a struggle and a contention for material existence that threatens to disorganize society, and render all the restraints of morality and religion utterly nugatory," a phenomenon such as spiritualism or a belief in spirits and ghosts becomes absolutely necessary, Crowe insists. Nor does she fail to note the special attraction of such a phenomenon to women. Classed among that "weak and foolish part of the world," truly at a disadvantage because they are not allowed to contend for their "material existence," finding their supposed moral and religious "influence" rendered "nugatory" by the very "struggle and contention for material existence," women, she implies, should be seers capable of pointing beyond that deadening materialism.[28]

To convince nineteenth-century skeptics of a world beyond mammon and matter, two English matrons wrote major books, published in the same year, faithfully recording and defending spiritual manifestations and powers. Sophia De Morgan's *From Matter to Spirit* is an informative

26. Ibid., 120; Black, *Notable Women Authors of the Day*, 89.
27. See Nancy Cott, *The Bonds of Womanhood: "Woman's Sphere" in New England, 1780–1835*, 137.
28. *Spiritualism and the Age We Live In*, 132, 131, 141.

work on the types and functions of the spiritual medium. Supposedly written at the behest of the spirits themselves, Emma Hardinge's *Modern American Spiritualism* proclaims the glories of the spiritualist movement while presenting a thorough record of the movement's progress in America. In their books De Morgan and Hardinge tried to accommodate the Victorian dualisms of insight and conception, darkness and light, intuition and reason. "Never has any way been made," states eminent mathematician and logician Professor Augustus De Morgan, in the preface to his wife's work, "by observation alone. Facts have sometimes started a theory; but until sagacity had conjectured, divined, guessed, surmised . . . what they pointed to, the facts were a mob, and not an army."[29] Both women called for a union between God as the preternatural agent of the soul's immortality and science as the ordering agent of matter. For Hardinge, spiritualism was a marriage of scientific reason and supernatural belief that yielded a spiritual science.

Sophia De Morgan not only felt that God was manifested in the progress from matter to spirit—"We [should not] undervalue the raps and movements, strange and childish as they appear: they form but the lowest step of a ladder whose base is on the earth, and whose top rests at the feet of the Lamb in the centre of the Throne"—but she also contended that incredible phenomena such as ghosts merited the attention of scientists as well as of theologians. Thus, in hopes that Victorian scientists and rationalists would find the preternatural phenomena more acceptable and credible, she sought a connection between spiritualism and the more objectively verifiable mesmerism. Hardinge, who likewise believed that science could substantiate the belief in God, declared, first, that "Chemistry, Physiology, Phrenology, Magnetism, and Clairvoyance" were all revealing precursors of nature's supernatural "mysteries," and, second, that the new spiritual science was "placing religion no longer on the foundations of fleeting human opinion, human assertion, or theory, but on the enduring basis of scientific facts."[30]

29. Preface to Sophia De Morgan, *From Matter to Spirit: The Result of Ten Years' Experience in Spirit Manifestations. Intended as a Guide to Enquirers*, xxiv.

30. De Morgan, *From Matter to Spirit*, 380; Hardinge, *Modern American Spiritualism: A Twenty Years' Record of the Communion between Earth and the World of Spirits*, 22, 520.

Paradoxically, the idea of engaging in intellectual or scientific discourse proved very attractive to women who believed in and wrote about the supernatural. As spiritual authorities of sorts, women conversant with the quasi-scientific or scientifically based mesmerism and spiritualism could finally set foot on turf that had been strictly off limits. As Nancy Tuana notes in her preface to *Feminism and Science,*

> The politics of science have included woman within the gaze of science but have excluded her from the practice of science. . . . To be a scientist one must be objective—woman is incapable of objectivity. A scientist makes rational judgements—woman is incapable of reason. A scientist desires truth—woman desires only truth's opposite, passion.
>
> This conception of woman's nature has excluded us from the very process of defining ourselves.

Dubbed angels in the house, Victorian women were even more notably "defined . . . out of science,"[31] but the emergence of supernaturalism as an important concern or interest of the age opened for women a window onto or a back door into the exclusive domain. Denied the possibility of being doctors, scientists, or priests, women writers such as De Morgan and Hardinge, in defining and underlining the supernatural experience with scientific as well as theological explanations, took a step from kitchen and boudoir not only toward the seminary but also toward the laboratory.

For the time being, however, the parlor served as seminary and laboratory for those women who were seers or mediums. These individuals drew the dead and the living into their parlors to hold séances that became so popular that even Queen Victoria participated in them. During these bewitching gatherings, tables rose and sometimes floated through the air; rappings or knockings were heard on various pieces of furniture and at different places in the room; and at times a spirit would inhabit the body of the medium to write, to draw, or, as in the case of the great Daniel Dunglas Home, to levitate through the air. In the midst of these supernatural happenings, women who had supposedly always exerted a subtle spiritual guidance in the home now, as seers and mediums, sat at the head of the table: they became acknowledged spiritual guides, supernaturally chosen disseminators of spiritualism.

31. *Feminism and Science,* vii.

In England, Eliza Finch, Florence Cook, Miss Fay, and Miss Chandos were a few of the more prominent mediums. One Miss Elizabeth Squirrell achieved such recognition of her visionary and spiritual powers that William Howitt, in his *History of the Supernatural*, pronounced her "The Seeress of Shottisham" in honorable emulation of the renowned Seeress of Prevorst. The first to introduce the séance into England was an American woman, a Mrs. Hayden, of whom a prominent English statesman was said to have declared that she "deserved a monument, if only for the conversion of Robert Owen." Herself a medium, Emma Hardinge cataloged the active female mediums in America, where spiritualism had been, according to Howitt, stronger than in England:

> Amongst the more distinguished professional or public mediums were Mrs. Coan, the excellent test rapping medium; George Redman, a rapping, writing, and test medium . . . Mrs. Cora Brown, Miss Middlebrook, and Miss Sarah Irish, admirable mediums for tests by rapping, seeing, writing, trance, etc.; Mrs. Bradley and Mrs. Townsend . . . Mrs. Kellog, one of the best clairvoyant, personating, seeing and writing mediums in the country; Mrs. Harriet Porter . . . Miss Seabring . . . Miss Mildred Cole, a child scarcely twelve years of age . . . the still famous Miss Leah Fish, of the Fox Family . . .

As this list indicates, the ranks of the spiritualist movement swelled with women: Mr. Redman seems buried among this heap of matrons and maidens. As Alex Owen put it in her groundbreaking study of British women and spiritualism, "The point is not that there were no spiritualist men but that, on the contrary, they have received a disproportionate amount of attention in serious accounts of spiritualism and the spiritualist movement." Many of the mediums who sat at the séance table were women because "women picked up the techniques of mediumship more rapidly and effectively than men, and they were often swift to move to the fore as developing mediums."[32] Then, too, having no public or professional face to save, women were no doubt less reluctant to engage in these unauthorized activities.

Supernaturalism indeed had an infectious appeal for those ladies who, despite the disapprobation of disbelieving husbands, doctors, and priests, persisted in their séances and supernatural beliefs. That the bitter

32. Hardinge, *Modern American Spiritualism*, 147, 149–50; Owen, *The Darkened Room*, 2, 5.

attacks of rationalists could not weaken the appeal suggests a special feminine rebellion that stemmed from deep-seated needs for action and self-expression, the urge to communicate, and the longing for public and professional recognition. By eagerly opening their minds to what the Seerees of Prevorst had called the inner life, female mediums and believers of the supernatural were making headway in their outer lives: being seen, heard, and studied. Then, too, spiritualism was a new area of knowledge in which women, for the most part, had outstripped the scientists. "Observation," wrote Crowe, is "a faculty, by the way, which our scientific men appropriate wholly to themselves. On this occasion, however, they have certainly yielded their pre-eminence to the 'weak and foolish' . . . for it is women and unscientific persons that have hitherto carried out these experiments, and satisfied themselves of their soundness."[33] Through spiritualism, mesmerism, and supernaturalism, the Victorian woman probed the nature and the extent of her spirituality and discovered expression, freedom, and power.

33. Crowe, *Spiritualism and the Age We Live In,* 138.

3

Spells and Dreams, Hollows and Moors

Supernaturalism in *Jane Eyre* and *Wuthering Heights*

$\mathcal{O}$N DECEMBER 13, 1847, three years after Harriet Martineau's miraculous mesmeric cure and nearly three months after the publication of *Jane Eyre*, Jane Welsh Carlyle, writing to her uncle John Welsh about "Harriet Martineau's outpourings in the 'Athenaeum,'" contemned mesmerism as "this devilish thing."[1] Conceding that what she had to say about the phenomenon was "not easy to say," she was "very sure" of one thing, "that the less one has to do with it the better." Carlyle's impulse was to deflate the significance of this scientific imposture by denying its originality. As far as she was concerned, "it [was] all of one family with witchcraft, demoniacal possession—[was], in fact, the selfsame principle presenting itself under new scientific forms, and under a polite name." Animal magnetism, or mesmerism as it was commonly called, was not to be denied, but it was not to be viewed as in any way revolutionary or wondrous:

---

1. "Letter 102," in *Letters and Memorials of Jane Welsh Carlyle*, 2:21–25; all references in this and the following paragraph are taken from these pages. Basham is very much attuned to the connection between witchcraft and mesmerism in *Trial of Woman*, in which she observes that mesmerism "occupies an interesting position in the history of nineteenth century occultism because of its ambivalent status, poised half way between a theological discourse with its suppressed demonologies of satanism and witchcraft, and new scientific paradigms of reality which would dialectically transform those demonologies into the Victorian concept of the New Woman" (75).

To deny that there is such a thing as animal magnetism, and that it actually does produce many of the phenomena here recorded, is idle; nor do I find much of this, which seems wonderful because we think of it for the first time, a whit more wonderful than those common instances of it, which never struck us with surprise merely because we have been used to see them all our lives. Everybody, for instance, has seen children thrown almost into convulsions by someone going through the motions of tickling them! Nay, one has known a sensitive uncle shrink his head between his shoulders at the first pointing of a finger towards his neck!

Does not a man physically tremble under the mere look of a wild beast or fellow-man that is stronger than himself? Does not a woman redden all over when she feels her lover's eyes on her? How then should one doubt the mysterious power of one individual over another? Or what is there more surprising in being made rigid than in being made red? in falling into sleep, than in falling into convulsions? in following somebody across a room, than in trembling before him from head to foot?

The equations she sets up for her uncle constitute the crux of Carlyle's argument, which essentially normalizes what has supernatural overtones. In other words, by pairing the blush with the rigidity of the mesmeric trance or convulsions with mesmeric sleep, Carlyle sought as much as was possible to bring animal magnetism within the realm of mundane as opposed to supernatural experience. If mesmerism was mysterious, it was commonly mysterious. That is, mesmerism partook of the common mysteries of human behavior, having none of the strangeness that lies beyond the pale of human understanding.

Fully convinced that no one "could be reduced to that state [of trance] without the consent of their own volition," Carlyle, who agreed to a mesmeric trial, was, like George Eliot and Charlotte Brontë, who would undergo similar trials, surprised when, as she recounts it, "flash there went over me, from head to foot, something precisely like what I once experienced from taking hold of a galvanic ball, only not nearly so violent." She got beyond this unsettling moment as she "had presence of mind to keep looking him [the mesmerist] in the face, as if I had felt nothing." Clearly the practical and levelheaded Carlyle was determined not to be impressed by what she perceived to be a "damnable sort of tempting of Providence, which I, as one solitary individual, will henceforth stand entirely aloof from." Martineau's "outpourings" were "humbug": "Poking into these mysteries of nature" was "not the result of superstitious ignorance, but of educated self-conceit."

Early on captivated by physiognomy and a phrenology that had often been linked to mesmerism, and finally exposed to the mesmeric experiments of her friend Harriet Martineau, Charlotte Brontë, unlike Martineau or Carlyle, was neither convinced nor incredulous, but something in between.[2] "You asked whether Miss Martineau made me a convert to mesmerism?" she wrote in 1851 to James Taylor. "Scarcely; yet I hear miracles of its efficacy and could hardly discredit the whole of what was told me. I even underwent a personal experiment; and though the result was not absolutely clear, it was inferred that in time I should prove an excellent subject."[3] In these brief comments on mesmerism, Brontë cautiously and diplomatically created with words and phrases such as "scarcely," "hardly discredit," and "not absolutely clear" a space for ambivalence and ambiguity. This ability to clear spaces was a tendency Brontë would put to great use in *Jane Eyre,* in which she employed tints of the supernatural to define the places the eponymous heroine of the novel comes to occupy in part because of physical, social, and spiritual differences that threaten to disable her in the realm of the mundane. In this novel about a penniless orphan girl who comes to assert her self and establish her independence in the face of guardians, teachers, and lover, retreats by the heroine into such enchanted places as moorland house, book, dream, art, mirror, and forest are retreats into equivocal, strange, indeterminate spaces where Brontë can more intensely and revealingly raise and address questions about the autonomy, will, and spirit of the female of whom society expects silence and sometimes the invisibility that comes of "fading into the woodwork." In *Jane Eyre,* Brontë ultimately wrote about her heroine's ghosthood.

Although it is not the first enchanted space in the novel, Moor House has the distinction of being the spot in the novel that Brontë most notably uses to experiment with what Carlyle sarcastically called the

2. See Chase's *Eros and Psyche* for a discussion of Brontë's "fascination with phrenology and physiognomy" (54–58) and a mention of the "great English exponent of Mesmerism . . . John Elliotson," who among other things founded in 1843 the *Zoist,* a "journal which promised a synthesis of phrenology and mesmerism" (105). In " 'The Mesmeric Mania': The Early Victorians and Animal Magnetism," Fred Kaplan also discusses the link between phrenology and animal magnetism, which "went hand in hand after 1838" (697).

3. Shorter, *The Brontës,* 2:192.

"new Gospel of Animal Magnetism." With its "humble kitchen," its "sanded," "scoured," "scrupulously clean," but unextraordinary appointments, with its rustic, "honest but inflexible" servant Hannah, its grim pastor and master St. John Rivers, and the "young, graceful," but initially undistinguishable ladies, the sisters of St. John, Mary and Diana, Moor House may seem one of the less enchanted spaces in the book.[4] However, Moor House proves as much of a spiritual crossroads as Whitcross—the place where Jane first disembarks from the coach that takes her from the love of her life, Mr. Rochester—is a physical crossroads, "where four roads meet" (*Eyre*, 284). As such it constitutes an ambiguous space for Jane, who arrives at Moor House looking "thin" and "bloodless," already a "mere spectre" (*Eyre*, 296). For at Moor House, or Marsh End as it is also called, Jane often finds herself in between. She is, for one thing, both excluded and included. Thus, when the servant Hannah— believing that any young woman who shows up on the moors at that time of night in the rain to beg for shelter and bread is not "what you ought to be"—shuts the door in the face of the starving, wandering Jane, St. John overturns that servant's harsh decision, admonishing, "Hush, Hannah! . . . You have done your duty in excluding, now let me do mine in admitting her" (*Eyre*, 295, 296). Later, however, after Jane has been not only admitted but also accepted as one of the family ("It seemed I had found a brother: one I could be proud of,—one I could love; and two sisters" [*Eyre*, 339]), it is St. John who excludes Jane by, for example, shaking her hand each night instead of administering the brotherly kiss he customarily gives to his sisters, then finally bestowing upon her kisses that are more ceremonious than brotherly or affectionate (*Eyre*, 350–51).

Moor House is the place where Jane wavers between her love for Rochester and the sense of duty that attaches her to St. John. Moor House is the place where she can physically recover from the privation and hardship of three days of aimless peregrinations on the moors without food or shelter; it is the place where Jane dares, in her own words, "put off the mendicant—to resume my natural manner and character" and begin "once more to know myself" (*Eyre*, 297). Yet this very house is a place where "this good man," St. John, is killing her in

4. Carlyle, *New Letters and Memorials of Jane Welsh Carlyle*, 1:158. Brontë, *Jane Eyre; An Authoritative Text, Backgrounds, Criticism*, 292, 295, 292; hereafter cited parenthetically as *Eyre*.

a vampiric draining of her happiness (*Eyre,* 362, 351, 363), where she experiences intense paroxysms of uncertainty (*Eyre,* 369), where she runs the risk of being halved ("Alas! If I join St. John, I abandon half myself" [*Eyre,* 356]; "to please him [St. John] . . . I must disown half my nature, stifle half my faculties, wrest my tastes from their original bent, force myself to the adoption of pursuits for which I had no natural vocation" [*Eyre,* 351]). Thus, although Jane declares while at Moor House that she knows "no medium: I never in my life have known any medium in my dealings with positive, hard characters, antagonistic to my own, between absolute submission and determined revolt," it is still correct to say that, at Moor House, Jane inhabits a space of intersection, of mediums, of "divided allegiance" (*Eyre,* 352, 357), of in-betweenness. Moreover, Moor House is where Jane Eyre comes to know firsthand the mediumship of mesmerism. For while the parson, St. John Rivers, whom Jane eventually discovers is her cousin, may espouse the Gospel of Christ, in his relations with Jane he tends to practice the "new Gospel of Animal Magnetism" as he presses Jane to marry him and live out her days in India with him as "the sole helpmeet [he] can influence efficiently in life and retain absolutely till death" (*Eyre,* 357).

Indeed, at Moor House the processes of mesmerism lend a special depth and meaning to Jane's interactions with St. John, whom Penny Boumelha describes as one who disposes, determines, and regulates: "Only the returning St. John . . . has the power to admit the beggar [Jane] into the house of gentlemen's children, and his first act is to acknowledge, but also to take control over, that unsatisfied appetite that has structured her [Jane's] narrative thus far."[5] It is only during her sojourn at Moor House that Jane, like a typical mesmeric subject, feels herself powerless as she stands before a male controller. "I felt," says Jane, recalling a conversation with St. John, "as if an awful charm was framing round and gathering over me: I trembled to hear some fatal word spoken which would at once declare and rivet the spell" (*Eyre,* 353–54). Time and time again Jane feels the force of St. John's mesmeric hold: "I shuddered as he spoke: I felt his influence in my marrow—his hold on my limbs" (*Eyre,* 357). St. John, Jane admits, "acquired a certain influence over me that took away my liberty of mind . . . I could no longer talk or

5. *Charlotte Brontë,* 69.

laugh freely when he was by . . . I fell under a freezing spell" (*Eyre*, 350). At one point, left alone with St. John, who was "deciphering his crabbed Oriental scrolls" while she herself sat reading Schiller, Jane glances at St. John only to succumb to his preternatural gaze: "There I found myself under the influence of the ever-watchful blue eye. How long it had been searching me through and through, and over and over, I cannot tell: so keen was it, and yet so cold, I felt for the moment superstitious—as if I were sitting in the room with something uncanny" (*Eyre*, 349). Of course what is really at stake here is power, control, and will. Jane feels herself "painfully controlled by [St. John's] will." The fact that he has an uncanny ability to immobilize Jane, no matter how temporarily, to freeze her will for a spell ("I, like a fool, never thought of resisting him—I could not resist him" [*Eyre*, 350, 352]), is indicative not only of the psychic energies flowing between Jane and her kinsman but also of how morally, not sexually, seductive and spiritually oppressive St. John could ultimately prove, if Jane should consent to marry him.

Not even Rochester, whom Jane loves, has been able to hold her so completely with the gaze of his eagle eye, though finally, having lost his sight, Rochester sends forth a supernatural call to Jane that breaks the "torpor" of the trancelike influence the "austere and despotic" (*Eyre*, 369, 360) St. John exerts over her. This is not to say that Rochester does not have his own "spell to attract" (*Eyre*, 154), for Rochester's "energy, decision, [and] will" both master and influence Jane too, but without the decided mesmeric allure of the panoptic eye. As Jane puts it, "He [Rochester] made me love him without looking at me" (*Eyre*, 153). The main point is that having brought her protagonist to Moor House and to a final consideration of consent, power, control, and will—all the components of her own energies—Charlotte Brontë represents this special leg of Jane's journey not in biblical but in mesmeric terms clearly meant to enhance the reader's comprehension of Jane's predicament. At this juncture of the novel, the mesmerism that was so much a topic of the day put at Brontë's disposal a stock of words and images that enabled her not only to portray more keenly the nuance between Jane and her cousin St. John but also to express more forcefully both the natural and the spiritual reality she had conceived for her heroine.

The mesmeric exchange between Jane and St. John lends support to Jane Carlyle's pragmatic contention that animal magnetism is no more wonderful than what happens when a woman reddens all over at the feel of her lover's eyes, that magnetism is no more or no less than the "mysterious power of one individual over another";[6] however, Brontë's repeated use of words like *spell, charm, shudder,* finally does just as much to naturalize or humanize the supernatural as it does to take the miracle out of the eerie phenomenon. One of the things that happens in *Jane Eyre* is that the unknowable, the transcendent, and the otherworldly can also find expression in one who is very much, if not fully, vested in this world. In the novel, Jane not only inhabits a series of lurid supernaturalized spaces but is herself represented as such a space. Thus, at Moor House, Jane undergoes a "specterization" in her relations with St. John, who sees but does not see his kinswoman. He, for instance, acknowledges "something brave in [her] spirit, as well as penetrating in [her] eye" (*Eyre,* 330); he detects "lines of force in her face" (*Eyre,* 299) and even identifies with her restlessness (*Eyre,* 310, 312). He observes closely her being. Yet no matter how much St. John, for whom the "humanities and amenities of life had no attraction" (*Eyre,* 345), gazes at Jane with his cold-blue instrumental eyes (*Eyre,* 304), he does not see her fully or completely. Half of her becomes invisible as he sets aside her flesh and her passion to define her in terms of energy he wishes to put at the disposal of patriarchy. Jane can neither show a fine hand, a delicate neck, or a comely arm that St. John can lust after or merely desire nor offer a heart he can love. She knows that though he will exact the physical privileges of a husband, he is not interested in her flesh or her humanity: "I will throw all on the altar—heart, vitals, the entire victim. He will never love me; but he shall approve me; I will show him energies," she concludes. One page later she yet again resolves, "I will give the missionary my energies—it is all he wants—but not myself" (*Eyre,* 356, 357).

For St. John, Jane is as present and absent as a ghost. He quickly determines that Jane is physically insubstantial and plain, though he does note her rather "unusual physiognomy." He pronounces her "sensible, but not at all handsome," a woman who "would always be plain," since the "grace and harmony of beauty are quite wanting in those features" (*Eyre,* 298, 299). But she has a force, drive, vitality he thinks will subserve

---

6. Interestingly enough, when St. John, Jane's would-be lover, having bestowed "an experiment kiss" on Jane, looks at her, Jane does not blush or redden as Carlyle's hypothetical woman does, but rather she "might have turned a little pale" (*Eyre,* 350).

his own ends. Holy man, mesmerizer, "strange being" (*Eyre*, 365) that he is, St. John has only a clue to the true depths of Jane's spirit and the force of her will. So even as he constructs her as a ghost of sorts, he cannot fully participate in her spiritual knowledge, though he expects her to share his. No wonder that when Jane feels what is "not like an electric shock; but . . . quite as sharp, as strange, as startling," St. John, who has laid "his shaping hand" on Jane's head, though not oblivious to what has transpired, is nevertheless unable to share or interpret the phenomenon correctly (*Eyre*, 369, 355). For though he ultimately suspects that Jane's need for love makes her weak, he is inclined to believe in the efficacy of his own powers. Consequently, St. John seems to believe that what amounts to a supernatural summons from Rochester is a near conversionary experience for Jane, or so the note he slips under her door the next morning indicates: "You left me too suddenly last night. Had you stayed but a little longer, you would have laid your hand on the Christian's cross and the angel's crown. I shall expect your clear decision when I return this day fortnight. Meantime, watch and pray that you enter not into temptation: the spirit, I trust, is willing, but the flesh, I see, is weak. I shall pray for you hourly,—Yours, St. John" (*Eyre*, 370).

As far as Jane is concerned, St. John knows but does not know her. She is more absent than present in his eyes. He and she are finally unable to share fully either the sympathies that humanize or the presentiments that transcend. These are the supernaturalisms or obscure "dynamisms"[7] that after all inform Jane's being and her experience: "Presentiments are strange things!" declares Jane, "and so are sympathies; and so are signs: and the three combined make one mystery to which humanity has not yet found the key. I never laughed at presentiments in my life; because I have had strange ones of my own. Sympathies, I believe, exist . . . whose workings baffle mortal comprehension. And signs, for aught we know, may be but the sympathies of Nature with man" (*Eyre*, 193). Aside from cultivating the ground for both her narration of the dreams that will haunt her and her discovery of her kinspeople at Moor House, Jane Eyre here bears witness to and thereby validates, even if she does not

7. I borrow the term *dynamism* from Rosalind Miles's "A Baby God: The Creative Dynamism of Emily Brontë's Poetry," in Harold Bloom, ed., *The Brontës*, 69–89.

vigorously endorse, a special reality at which others may be tempted to laugh. She, however, receives this reality in great earnestness, having "never laughed at presentiments in my life; because I have had strange ones of my own."

To be laughed at, to have one's experiences and beliefs scoffed at, would constitute just one more form of rejection in a novel deeply concerned with rejection: "Why was I always suffering, always brow-beaten, always accused, for ever condemned?" wails ten-year-old Jane. "Why could I never please? Why was it useless to try to win anyone's favour?" (*Eyre*, 12). The most compelling response to Jane's questions is the notion of difference. The people around Jane tend to look at her and, missing her spirit, see in her person one who, unlike themselves, is plain, poor, and unprepossessing.

In her preface to *Jane Eyre*, Charlotte Brontë deplores the superficial valuations of those who too often confound appearance and truth and find "it convenient to make external show pass for sterling worth."[8] It is just this sort of seeing or inability to see that makes Jane an insubstantial and spectral figure in the world of the Reeds and Ingrams, even as Jane herself voluntarily turns herself over to spectralness. Thus, "shrined in [the] double retirement" of a recessed window seat hidden by "the red moreen curtain" (*Eyre*, 5), orphaned little Jane Eyre makes herself invisible as she secures not the Bible, a conventional source of solace and retreat for conventional souls, but Bewick's *History of British Birds,* a natural volume suited to the supernaturalized flight in which Jane, a spritelike young girl bound to a dreary existence, needs to engage. With this special volume she enters "forlorn regions of dreary space" where she finds a "cold and ghastly moon glancing through bars of cloud," "marine phantoms," and "the fiend pinning down the thief's pack behind him" (*Eyre*, 6). Banished from the drawing room at Gateshead, Jane finds these twilight regions a welcome alternative because they provide a wordless translation of the dimly understood reality within. "Each picture told a story; mysterious often to my undeveloped understanding and imperfect feelings, yet ever profoundly interesting" (*Eyre*, 6). The eerie pictures Jane finds in Bewick's *History* dramatically record the shadows and solitary places in a soul that is not as dull as some would

8. Preface to *Jane Eyre*, 1–2.

make it out to be. The truth is that no one at Gateshead knows how "profoundly interesting" the physically and economically inferior Jane is. Few will know at Thornfield, as Brontë puts it in her preface to the posthumously published *The Professor*, what "agitates divers souls that show a calm and sober surface."9

Jane proves impenetrable, if not invisible, when later in the novel Rochester reviews the watercolors she had made at Lowood school. These paintings of a sea, sky, and polar scape, which Jane saw "with the spiritual eye, before I attempted to embody them," are, in spite of the artist's modest protests that they are "pale portrait[s] of the thing I had conceived" (*Eyre*, 110), "wonderful" and "startling"10 because the tints and the subjects—"a drowned corpse glanc[ing] through the green water," the Evening Star represented as "rising into the sky . . . a woman's shape to the bust," and "a colossal head, inclined towards [an] iceberg" (*Eyre*, 110)—are not exactly the stuff of this world. So Rochester declares:

> As to the thoughts, they are elfish. These eyes in the Evening Star you must have seen in a dream. How could you make them look so clear, and yet not at all brilliant? for [*sic*] the planet above quells their rays. And what meaning is that in their solemn depth? And who taught you to paint wind? There is a high gale in that sky, and on this hilltop. Where did you see Latmos? For that is Latmos. There,—put the drawings away!
> (*Eyre*, 111)

Like St. John, Rochester sees some things but cannot see others. He is able to identify, for instance, Latmos, a mountain located in what is now Turkey; however, he is surprised to learn that Jane can picture this sign of latent sexuality, this place where the moon goddess Selene is said to have visited Endymion and kissed him into eternal sleep. The impenetrability of Jane's drawings is marked by Rochester's rapid-fire questions and his impatient command that the drawings be put away. He obviously finds these works as disconcerting as they are difficult to interpret. The barrage of questions remains unanswered and is not meant to be answered. Instead the questions are meant to evoke the ineffable

9. Brontë [Currer Bell], *The Professor: A Tale*, vi; hereafter cited parenthetically as *Professor*.

10. I borrow the words *wonderful* and *startling* from Brontë herself, who wrote that even the most rational and sensible of beings, "men in business," have "casket[ed]" in their souls "a preference for the wild, wonderful, and thrilling—the strange, startling, and harrowing" (*Professor*, vi).

mystery of Jane's spirituality, even as they reveal Rochester's growing awareness that the being who created these strange pictures, these "prose fantas[ies]" as Ellen Moers terms them,[11] is not easily defined. Like the staid, commonplace, but mysterious Grace Poole, Jane herself is possessed of an "absolute impenetrability [that] is past comprehension" (*Eyre*, 134). Attracted to this dimension of Jane, Rochester—unable, as his questions indicate, to know her analytically—intuitively grasps the essence of Jane by assigning her to the realm of supernaturally empowered creatures who inhabit this earth. To Rochester, Jane is witch, sprite, changeling, and elf (*Eyre*, 131, 215).

The watercolors in the tradition of Bewick are the occasion for another of Jane's retreats into the otherworldly, as "art came to be," according to Daniel Cottom, "the legitimate supernatural in that it was understood to be the proper medium for the exercise of the powers traditionally attributed to the supernatural. In art one could manipulate human destinies, make people appear and disappear, see into the minds of others, hear the voices of the dead, levitate above this earth . . . and yet proceed under the assumption that the results represented ordinary nature."[12]

Although these forays into a supernaturalized art indicative of a nature that is finally anything but ordinary are not always unattended by anxiety, they prove increasingly familiar, restorative, and consolatory. "With Bewick on my knee, I was then happy: happy at least in my way," recalls Jane (*Eyre*, 7). Later she responds in a similar fashion to Rochester's query about her state of mind when she painted the watercolors. "Were you happy when you painted these pictures?" asks a baffled Rochester. "I was absorbed, sir: yes, and I was happy," is Jane's reply. "To paint them, in short, was to enjoy one of the keenest pleasures I have ever known" (*Eyre*, 111). This surprisingly strong statement is a tribute not merely to the gratification of artistic expression but more precisely to the manifestation of Jane's own spirituality. As these two flights into visionary hollows indicate, Jane's happiness will not be the happiness of those who can manage the social prescription of "a more sociable and childlike disposition, a more attractive and sprightly manner" (*Eyre*, 5).

11. *Literary Women*, 283.
12. *Abyss of Reason: Cultural Movements, Revelations, and Betrayals*, 94.

As a woman, Jane will neither search for happiness nor find her truth in the drawing rooms where the Georgiana Reeds and Blanche Ingrams languish and preside nor in the religion so necessary to Eliza Reed, so comforting to Helen Burns. The truth and sometimes the happiness Jane discovers in her "own way" lie in supernaturalized clearings that allow the development, the expansion, and the movement of what remains unseen and unappreciated by the characters in the novel who are "not quick either of vision or conception" (*Eyre*, 7)—Jane's spirit.

One of the most significant supernatural sites in the novel is the looking glass in the red room at Gateshead. When Jane first notices the mirror in the tomblike red room she sees only an impenetrable surface that merely "repeated" other surfaces; however, when she stands before the looking glass she begins to understand its spiritual dimension. For the "great looking-glass" is more than a flat surface. A mirror or looking glass can be, according to Jenijoy La Belle, "a male-directed instrument of literal objectification," part of a "limiting syndrome." But as La Belle adds, a writer such as French feminist Luce Irigaray does "not reject its [the mirror's] possibilities." La Belle, in her study of the looking glass, concedes that the mirror can be "useful," that it can be, in the hands of women, "a more flexible tool." In the hands of Charlotte Brontë, the red room's mirror offers not so much a "scene of nonrecognition," as La Belle contends, as it does a scene of exploration and of discovery.[13] The looking glass is what Jane calls it—a "visionary hollow," a plane of wonder with a depth that can reveal truth if one passes through to the other side. What it reveals to Jane is the reality of her own ghostliness: "All looked colder and darker in that visionary hollow than in reality: and the strange little figure there gazing at me, with a white face and arms specking the gloom, and glittering eyes of fear moving where all else was still, had the effect of a real spirit" (*Eyre*, 11).

In the looking glass, one can discover real spirits, ghosts, selves. Recalling Lewis Carroll's Alice in *Through the Looking Glass,* Nina Auerbach

13. *Herself Beheld: The Literature of the Looking Glass,* 179, 180, 138. La Belle finds Jane's crossing of the mirror "deeply disturbing" as "it demonstrates a division, with potentially pathogenic dimensions." La Belle's description of an "insurrection against the reflection" does not satisfactorily account for Jane's fascination with the "visionary hollow." In the mirror scene, Jane does not prove so much a stranger to herself as one who acknowledges her strangeness and recognizes her own ghostliness. Almost immediately upon looking into the mirror, Jane experiences "a rapid rush of retrospective thought" (*Eyre*, 11) that reveals her ghostly otherness.

comments that, after all, "It is the nature of the girl to fall through her looking glass into selfhood." Auerbach, who observes that Alice becomes a queen, grants Jane Eyre, "in her own stern way," this same distinction. However, Jane is finally less a queen than "the eerie figure she sees properly for the first time" in the mirror, a ghost. In what Auerbach calls the "vision of her own unrealized depths," Jane ultimately outdistances Carroll's Alice, who must dream in order to find the wonder of self, while Jane sees directly, in "a flash of sacred terror," as Auerbach puts it, "the realization of her powers," the wonder of her self.[14]

Jane is not completely unlike another, older Alice created by Irigaray in "The Looking Glass, from the Other Side." Both Brontë's Jane and Irigaray's Alice provide instances, to borrow La Belle's words, of "a female looking into [a mirror] and thinking about how she looks and who she is," a female "search[ing] deeply into hidden caverns of female selfhood."[15] Like Carroll's Alice, both Brontë's Jane and Irigaray's Alice know about or experience "fabulous, fantastic, unbelievable things." Jane and the older Alice have not simply imagined or intuited, they have seen their identities—that is to say, they have traveled "behind the screen of representation" to discover "Difference," as Irigaray would put it, "always in displacement" (*This Sex*, 12, 9, 16), difference that is not necessarily negative.[16]

What Jane sees behind the screen is her soul's greatest desire and its greatest fear, which finally are so blurred that they are, to borrow Irigaray's words, not easily "distinguished" or "differentiated" (*This Sex*, 10). For Jane's ultimate desire is to experience not just sexual but spiritual communion with someone who will not be an eternal stranger. This desire for what Jane herself calls "fellow-feeling" (*Eyre*, 13) in turn defines her fear, which is the only thing that pulses in that "visionary

14. *Private Theatricals*, 27, 26.

15. "The Looking Glass, from the Other Side" is in Irigaray's *This Sex Which Is Not One*; hereafter cited parenthetically as *This Sex*. La Belle, *Herself Beheld*, 12, 180.

16. In "This Essentialism Which Is Not One: Coming to Grips with Irigaray," Naomi Schor explains how Irigaray "exposes" that which would "den[y] the objectified other the right to her difference" (65). In *God between Their Lips: Desire between Women in Irigaray, Brontë, and Eliot*, Kathryn Bond Stockton uncovers "connections . . . between post-structuralists and Victorians" and argues that Irigaray is a "hinge between post-structuralist feminists and Victorian women novelists," an unconscious "heir to Victorian traditions," or better yet "a relevant . . . consummation of them." Irigaray's spirituality, as Stockton describes it, is not related to ghosts or to the supernatural, but rather to the body and the "slide between opacity, lack, and labor" (xvi, xviii, xxiii, xx).

hollow," rendering it "colder and darker" than in reality, a fear that she will be alone, an eternal stranger to others and a stranger to herself. Thus, when Jane does look into the looking glass where she expects to find familiarity ("familiar to me as my own face in a glass" [*Eyre*, 177]), she discovers her own difference, a difference so stark that it belongs to the realm of ghostly lore: "I thought *it* like one of the tiny phantoms, half fairy, half imp, Bessie's evening stories represented as coming out of lone, ferny dells in moors, and appearing before the eyes of belated travellers" (*Eyre*, 11; my italics).

At the pinnacle of her isolation and separation, Jane Eyre, locked up in the room "remote from the nursery and kitchens" (*Eyre*, 11), and so denied the physical space of the rest of the house and denied even the meager company of the servant woman Bessie—Jane Eyre, so circumstanced, experiences a "space warp" that she herself inhabits as a ghost. Feminist philosopher Mary Daly sheds yet more light on Jane's spectrally mirrored transformation when she notes, "Denial of physical space is accompanied by overt and subtle levels of denial of mental and emotional space. Since these space warps are so invisible and subliminal, women struggling under such conditions often feel 'spacy,' or dis-oriented. This effect is increased by the fact that women are spatially separated from each other on many levels—forced into conditions of isolation and alienation which are felt as ghostly, spooky."[17] If Daly's account of female ghosthood is admitted, the mirror then not only frames young Jane's alienation but also allows her to imbue her markedly physical incarceration with all its emotional and spiritual significance and to assess it accordingly.

By her own admission fascinated but disturbed by the ghost in the great looking glass, Jane "returned to my stool" (*Eyre*, 11), where she does on the outside of the looking glass something very similar to what Irigaray's Alice does on the other side: she seizes the moment and "come[s] on stage herself. With her violet, violated eyes. Blue and red. Eyes that recognize the right side, the wrong side, and the other side: the blur of deformation; the black or white of a loss of identity" (*This Sex*, 10). Jane's eyes may not be violet or even hazel, as Rochester later mistakenly assumes, but they are at this point violated with scenes

17. *Pure Lust: Elemental Feminist Philosophy*, 18.

of "All John Reed's violent tyrannies, all his sisters' proud indifference, all his mother's aversion, all the servants' partiality" (*Eyre*, 11). Her (in fact green) eyes are figuratively blue with the hurt of longing to please, to win anyone's favor, to be respected, and to receive the most meager indulgence; they are red with the violence of her emotions: "my blood was still warm . . . 'Unjust!—unjust!' said my reason, forced by the agonising stimulus into precocious though transitory power. . . . What a consternation of soul was mine that dreary afternoon! How all my brain was in tumult, and all my heart in insurrection!" (*Eyre*, 11–12). Like Alice, Jane will at last come to see all sides of her predicament, "the right side, the wrong, and the other side":

> now, at the distance of—I will not say how many years, I see it clearly.
> I was a discord in Gateshead Hall; I was like nobody there; I had nothing in harmony with Mrs. Reed or her children, or her chosen vassalage. If they did not love me, in fact, as little did I love them. They were not bound to regard with affection a thing that could not sympathise with one amongst them; a heterogeneous thing, opposed to them in temperament, in capacity, in propensities; a useless thing, incapable of serving their interest, or adding to their pleasure; a noxious thing, cherishing the germs of indignation at their treatment, of contempt of their judgement. (*Eyre*, 12)

In this passage Jane presents the Reeds' as well as her own perspective and, by doing so, sees her own social powerlessness (she is unsympathetic, heterogeneous, useless, incapable) and yet her own power to grant or to withhold her affections: "If they did not love me, in fact, as little did I love them."

It is fitting that, having harshly if realistically and honestly painted herself, as she literally does in narrating the novel, the "uncongenial alien permanently intruded" upon the well-fleshed and monied Reeds of Gateshead Hall, young Jane finds her thoughts flowing toward the opposite extreme. For, turning "a fascinated eye towards the dimly gleaming mirror," the scorned child raises the ghost of her Uncle Reed who, had he lived, "would have treated me kindly." Jane's turn to the mirror and to thoughts of her dead uncle constitutes yet another retreat into another world. But again, once Jane comes to that world, desire and fear are hard to separate, for while the idea of the ghostly visitation is "consolatory in theory, I felt [it] would be terrible if realised" (*Eyre*, 13).

While no ghostly visitation is literally realized in the novel, at a figurative level Jane Eyre, who has had occasion to glance around and "make sure that nothing worse than myself haunted the shadowy room" (*Eyre*, 23–24), is indeed akin to the ghost. For like a ghost whose displacement constitutes having a place in two worlds or having no permanent place in either world, Jane is truly the *geist*, ghost or guest. As ward, teacher, governess, lover, and long-lost kinswoman in the several houses she visits, she finds no "place" from which to center herself.[18] Although with each of the successive moves from Gateshead to Lowood to Thornfield to Moor House, Jane herself increasingly understands and correctly gauges the individuals she meets, others do not clearly perceive her. The Reeds, for example, think Jane an inferior being at Gateshead. At Lowood the uniform life the school offers does not ultimately satisfy the Jane who deep down needs action. Even Rochester, who is intellectually, emotionally, and socially more intimate with Jane than is any other character in the novel, shows an insensitivity to Jane's spirit when he presses her to deck herself out in the jewels and finery of a peer's daughter and offers her a life as his mistress when he cannot make her his wife. And, as we have seen, at Moor House, St. John, seeing clearly that part of Jane that is restless for action, cannot perceive her need for love.

Never seen fully, truly, or completely, the truth of her being remains as unseen and yet as present as a ghost. Unsurprisingly, Jane is more ghostlike when she is at Gateshead, where for the Reeds the very sight of Jane proves irritating. Her physical appearance precludes the Reeds' vision of the essential Jane, who, the reader is to understand, has for the most part proved passive and invisible in much the same way as another of Charlotte Brontë's characters, Lucy Snowe of *Villette*. On one occasion Jane "materializes," as it were, asserting and expressing the truth of her inner being in an ultimately bloody flash of ire directed at her cousin John that forces those at Gateshead to take note of her. But even these revelatory moments confirm Jane's utter difference, displacing her into the realm of one who is paradoxically a part of and yet does not belong to their world. As a result, until she meets Rochester, Jane wanders in a world where she has little or no power to "*charm*" or "influence" (*Eyre*, 164). "I still felt as a wanderer on the face of the earth; but I experienced

18. See Tony Tanner's ideas on home in his introduction to Charlotte Brontë's *Villette*, 12–29.

firmer trust in myself and my own powers, and less withering dread of oppression" (*Eyre*, 200).

What Jane does have is the capacity to haunt people as surely and as effectively as "Grace Poole—that living enigma, that mystery of mysteries"—haunts Jane herself at Thornfield (*Eyre*, 178). Like Grace, Jane is a recurring subject of eerie curiosity, a "queer" (*Eyre*, 33) being whose behavior and presence often baffle expectations and the established or recognized order of things. At Gateshead, for example, the "unchildlike" Jane spooks the worldly Mrs. Reed as "something spoke out of me over which I had no control" (*Eyre*, 210, 23). Like one possessed, Jane invokes the spirit of Mr. Reed: "What would uncle Reed say to you, if he were still alive?" (*Eyre*, 23). So shaken and reduced is Mrs. Reed, whose "usually cold composed grey eye became troubled with a look like fear" (*Eyre*, 23), that she calls in the clergyman Brocklehurst, who is to exorcise Jane by enrolling her at Lowood school, which he directs. Years after Jane has been routed from the walls of Gateshead, we learn that she has still been a torment to Mrs. Reed, who calls Jane back on her deathbed to say that she has been haunted: she "could not forget" Jane and the way she conducted herself as one possessed, as one she could "never comprehend" (*Eyre*, 210).

Interestingly enough, Rochester even more strongly confirms Jane's ghostliness when she returns from the home of her now dead and buried aunt. For him, Jane "steal[s] into the vicinage of your home [Thornfield] along with twilight, just as if you were a dream or a shade." When he asks what Jane has been doing for the last month, Jane's reply that she has been with her "aunt, sir, who is dead," lends itself to Rochester's bantering and yet meaningful insistence that Jane is a ghost to him, present and yet not present, here and yet beyond his grasp, neither available to him nor, as her watercolors have shown, always comprehensible: "Good angels be my guard!" cries Rochester, "She comes from the other world—from the abode of people who are dead; and tells me so when she meets me alone here in the gloaming! If I dared, I'd touch you, to see if you are substance or shadow, you elf!—but I'd as soon offer to take hold of a blue *ignis fatuus* light in a marsh" (*Eyre*, 215). The progression of Rochester's imprecise but fluid description from the supernatural ghost to the elf, that entity between supernatural and natural, to the *ignis fatuus,* a natural phenomenon, shows Rochester's linguistic attempt to bring Jane closer to earth and so within his reach even as it demonstrates that, like the ghost, the character of Jane does not move in one plane of existence. She is a richer and more exceptional character because she belongs not only to the natural realm of the *ignis fatuus* but also to the supernatural realm of shadow, realms diametrically opposed to Blanche's and Mrs. Reed's utilitarian world of money, bulk, and status.

Near the end of the novel, with its diversity of supernatural spaces, Jane has inherited twenty thousand pounds and so gained that substance calculated to lend her social visibility or prominence in the materialistic world. Brontë, however, maintains, even if tenuously, Jane's ghostly allure, removing her character from society to the natural though rather isolated or buried world of a dense forest.[19] When Jane steps from the dense woods into the semicircular clearing of Ferndean she does so as a ministrant spirit or a ghost. Rochester's blasted sight makes, as Jane says, "myself unseen, and alas! to him invisible" (*Eyre*, 379). Fearing that Jane will again desert him, Rochester notes Jane's apparition-like faculty for "passing like a shadow, whither and how to me unknown; and for me remaining afterwards undiscoverable" (*Eyre*, 385). He indirectly insists on her supernatural dimension: "You are altogether a human being, Jane? You are certain of that?" (*Eyre*, 385). When Jane and Rochester discuss one of "the strange[st] point[s]," the mysterious midnight summons, Jane's reaction proves itself strange, guarded, enigmatic: "I listened to Mr. Rochester's narrative; but made no disclosure in return. The coincidence struck me as too awful and inexplicable to be communicated or discussed. If I told anything, my tale would be such as must necessarily make a profound impression on the mind of my hearer: and that mind, yet from its sufferings too prone to gloom, needed not the deeper shade of the supernatural. I kept these things then, and pondered them in my heart" (*Eyre*, 394).

Jane's decision not to confirm with her own narrative the supernatural has several meanings. First, this withholding of information gives her a kind of power over Rochester, for her decision not to disclose the

19. Jane's removal to Ferndean is adumbrated in Rochester's promise to whisk Jane away to a fairy cave on the moon. The tale Rochester concocts for Adele veils the conditions of his marriage to Jane. "I must go with it [the fairy, Jane Eyre] out of the common world to a lonely place—such as the moon" or, as it turns out, Ferndean (*Eyre*, 235).

knowledge she has not only deprives him of that knowledge but also casts Jane as one who determines what and how much Rochester will know. Blinded, Rochester depends on Jane to help him see; therefore, she has the power to make a "profound impression." Her determination that Rochester "needed not the deeper shade of the supernatural" positions her as a mediator between Rochester and the supernatural. At this point she is physically and spiritually in charge and able to keep "these things" to herself, to appropriate them and ponder "them in my heart." Jane's odd decision not to tell Rochester that she had literally heard his mesmeric call across the miles marks Brontë's careful and light mining of the supernaturalism of nature and of mesmerism to create a mode by which she could embrace the different and the alien and limn the force of a woman's psyche, and her soul.

Jane's reticence about Rochester's mesmeric call also marks a restraint and caution that typify Charlotte Brontë's handling of supernaturalism. She had earlier wrangled with the subject in both her preface to her sister Emily's *Wuthering Heights* and her preface to her own *The Professor.* "If it was complained that the mere hearing of certain vivid and fearful scenes banished sleep by night," wrote Brontë, using the pseudonym Currer Bell, "and disturbed mental peace by day, Ellis Bell [Emily Brontë] would wonder what was meant, and suspect the complainant of affectation."[20] When Charlotte Brontë edited *Wuthering Heights* in 1850, she believed her sister Emily had been oblivious not only to what others read as the book's questionable morality but also to its powerful and integral supernaturalism. The book's moral and its supernatural elements are after all inextricably combined. The "rude and strange" ("Editor's Preface," 9) of the novel are vested in its supernaturalism, as one of Nelly's ponderings about one of the rudest and strangest of the novel's central characters, Heathcliff, clearly indicates: "Is he a ghoul, or a vampire?" wonders Nelly, "I had read of such hideous, incarnate demons."[21] Charlotte, who would praise the novel for being wonderfully "moorish, and wild, and knotty as a root of heath" ("Editor's Preface,"

---

20. Charlotte Brontë, "Editor's Preface," 10–11; hereafter cited parenthetically as "Editor's Preface."
21. Emily Brontë, *Wuthering Heights: Revised, An Authoritative Text with Essays in Criticism,* 260; hereafter cited parenthetically as *Heights.*

10), nevertheless, in the final words of her preface, like Nelly Dean, recoiled, though unwittingly, from a creation as awesome as it was awful:

> "Wuthering Heights" was hewn in a wild workshop, with simple tools, out of homely materials. The statuary found a granite block on a solitary moor: gazing thereon, he [Emily Brontë] saw how from the crag might be elicited a head, savage, swart, sinister; a form moulded with at least one element of grandeur—power. He wrought with a rude chisel, and from no model but the vision of his meditations. With time and labour, the crag took human shape; and there it stands colossal, dark, and frowning, half statue, half rock: in the former sense, terrible and goblin-like; in the latter, almost beautiful . . . ("Editor's Preface," 12)

Charlotte Brontë scripts her sister's literary labor as Frankensteinian. This is to say, Emily's creative act, as Charlotte describes it in this passage, mirrors that of Mary Shelley's Victor Frankenstein, the protagonist in what is, for all its Gothic aspects, arguably one of the earliest nineteenth-century ghost stories.[22] Emily's workshop is the moor, Victor's the laboratory; Emily's material is here "a granite block," Victor's dead bodies. Although the materials and workshops differ, Emily Brontë and Victor Frankenstein both create a titanic "human shape" with "a head, savage, swart, sinister." Charlotte surely felt that Emily had created such a Shelleyan monster in Heathcliff and that this "goblin-like" creature had flawed her sister's work. "Had she but lived," Charlotte hastens to assure the readers of the 1850 preface, "her mind would of itself have grown like a strong tree, loftier, straighter, wider-spreading, and its matured fruits would have attained a mellower ripeness and sunnier bloom" ("Editor's Preface," 11).

In her own first novel, *The Professor,* written contemporaneously with *Wuthering Heights,* Charlotte Brontë eschewed the supernatural. The closest this novel comes to presenting ghosts occurs in chapter 23. Here, the hero awakens from a troubled sleep and, like Job "when a spirit passed before his face," feels "the hair of . . . [his] flesh . . . [stand]

---

22. See Vanessa D. Dickerson, "The Ghost of a Self: Female Identity in Mary Shelley's *Frankenstein.*" Shelley anticipated the Victorian probing of the relation between science and the supernatural in *Frankenstein,* in which her monster, brought to life as it were in a scientific attic or laboratory, by his very presence as well as his murderous actions, makes of the women in the novel occulted figures. See also Basham's *Trial of Woman,* 5.

up": "A horror of great darkness fell upon me; I felt my chamber invaded by one I had known formerly, but had thought forever departed" (*Professor*, 281). By describing her hero's bout with hypochondria in supernatural terminology, Brontë tried to capitalize on the energy and emotion the supernatural can stir. It is a ploy she used later and more successfully in *Villette*, in which the specter of a nun turns out to be a lover lusting for his unangelic lover. Although drawn toward a quasi-biblical supernaturalism in *The Professor*, Charlotte Brontë never allowed it any autonomy: "That sound, and the sensation of chill anguish accompanying it, many would have regarded as supernatural; but I recognised it at once as the effect of reaction" (*Professor*, 281).

While *Wuthering Heights* eventually found a publisher in 1847, *The Professor* was consistently rejected and not published until 1857, after Charlotte Brontë's death. Whether or not Emily's use of supernaturalism made her novel more appealing to publishers than Charlotte's avoidance of it in her first novel remains a worthwhile speculation. Certainly in the preface to *The Professor*, Charlotte Brontë publicly announced her recognition of the power and the importance of the "wild, wonderful, and thrilling—the strange, startling, and harrowing" (*Professor*, vi). She had anticipated an audience whose literary thirsts could be assuaged by "a mixed and moderate cup of enjoyment," a realistic moderation that she offers in the simple story of an unassuming young man who works, gets married, and continues to work. "I find," she wrote perhaps a bit caustically, "the publishers in general scarcely approved of this system, but would have liked something more imaginative and poetical— something more consonant with a highly-wrought fancy, with a taste for pathos, with sentiments more tender, elevated, unworldly" (*Professor*, vi). Although she had sent the book out into a literary scene that was beginning to be dominated by realism, she had found that publishers were catering to readers who were not only beginning, as utilitarian and practical people, to attend lectures on geology and political economy, but who also—like the intellectual Harriet Martineau, the good doctor and president of the Phrenological Society John Elliotson, and the popular writer Charles Dickens—were fascinated by the uncanny, by phrenology, by mesmerism, by ghosts.

Both *Jane Eyre* and *Wuthering Heights* are wild cards in the nineteenth-century British literary stack of realistic novels. They portray female protagonists who "do not," as Harold Bloom argues, "fit into the grand array of heroines of the Protestant will that commences with Richardson's Clarissa Harlowe and goes through Austen's Emma Woodhouse and Fanny Price to triumph in George Eliot's Dorothea Brooke and Henry James's Isabel Archer." Bloom in essence has trouble placing the Brontës' novels squarely in the realistic tradition. J. Hillis Miller, however, writing about the more radical *Wuthering Heights*, manages to do so with little difficulty: "In spite of its many peculiarities of narrative technique and theme, it is, in its extreme vividness of circumstantial detail, a masterwork of 'realistic' fiction. It obeys most of the conventions of Victorian realism, though no reader can miss the fact that it gives these conventions a twist. The reader is persuaded that the novel is an accurate picture of the material and sociological conditions of life in Yorkshire in the early nineteenth century."[23]

In fact, *Jane Eyre* and *Wuthering Heights*, which have, between them, been described as High Romantic, Gothic, Marxist, as well as Realistic, are hard to pin down, critically ineffable; these "remarkable oddit[ies]," to borrow a phrase from Derek Traversi, refuse to solidify, materialize, or be particularized as one thing or another. Their effect is easily felt, but not so easily or conventionally seen or named. Not only are these texts about ghosts in the red room, in the mirror, and on the moors, they are ghostly texts whose meanings fall somewhere in the in-between. *Wuthering Heights* and its author especially lend themselves to the mysterious and the supernatural. Although no critic has read Emily Brontë's novel strictly as a ghost story, scholars who have found not only the book a "strange" work that "resists rational reduction to some principle of explanation" but also Emily's life a shrouded chapter of sorts, yielding few and meager details—these scholars have been more ready to concede the text's and the writer's association, if not communion, with the weird, the marvelous, the uncanny.[24] In *Wuthering Heights*,

23. Bloom, introduction to Bloom, ed., *The Brontës*, 2; Miller, "*Wuthering Heights*: Repetition and the Uncanny," in Bloom, ed., *The Brontës*, 169.

24. Traversi, "The Brontë Sisters and *Wuthering Heights*," in Thomas A. Vogler, ed., *Twentieth Century Interpretations of "Wuthering Heights*," 49. Charlotte Brontë wrote that her sister's book "might appear a rude and strange production" to those "who knew nothing of the author" ("Editor's Preface," 9). For an exploration of the idea of the uncanny, see Miller's "*Wuthering Heights*," in Bloom, ed., *The Brontës*, 169–92. Miller describes *Wuthering Heights* as made up of repetitions that "resist" realist interpretations or at least "theoretical domination" (177) and quite astutely suggests that this

Emily Brontë, unlike her sister Charlotte, deals unabashedly with the supernatural as liberation and just expression of the self.

Emily Brontë was especially suited for her bolder presentation of the supernatural, as the studies of biographers and critics have suggested. In *A Life of Emily Brontë,* for instance, Edward Chitham highlights a moment in which Charlotte Brontë's lifelong friend Ellen Nussey recalls how Patrick Brontë's supernatural yarns affected Emily: "Looking back on this visit, Ellen felt sure that one root of *Wuthering Heights* was in Mr Brontë's ghoulish stories. They made one 'shiver and shrink from hearing; but they were full of grim humour and interest to Mr Brontë and his children.'" While Nussey for her part was "terrified" by these "sessions," Emily Brontë's reaction to them was notably odd. Citing Brontë's first biographer, A. M. F. Robinson, Chitham reports that on one such occasion Brontë "wore a strange expression, gratified, pleased, as though she had gained something which seemed to complete a picture in her mind." Brontë's reported sphinxlike expression suggests that her father's "ghoulish stories" were more than pleasant little episodes, that they struck some deeper chord in Brontë, who after all as an adult would have mystical if not ghoulish experiences of her own. In fact, Brontë's own life story remains as perplexing as her reaction to Reverend Brontë's spooky stories. Vague and incomplete, records of her life at best present us only an apparition. To those who knew her or have studied her life, poetry, and fiction, from her sister Charlotte to Elizabeth Gaskell and from Clement Shorter to F. R. Leavis to Rosalind Miles, she has remained "strange," "reticent," "remote," "mystical," essentially unseen, a hauntingly vital presence. One critic opens her study of Emily Brontë's occulted life thus: "The life of Emily Brontë is shrouded in mystery, and she remains an elusive and mysterious figure, despite the efforts of her latest and most scrupulous biographer."[25] Charlotte Brontë may have valued mystery, but Emily Brontë was and remains a mystery.

Understandably, the supernaturalism in *Jane Eyre* and *Wuthering Heights* differs as radically as English garden and northern moor, mirror

---

resistance invites "a supernatural transcendent 'cause' for all events" (176). Rosalind Miles notes "Emily Brontë's strangeness, her remoteness . . . her reticence" ("A Baby God," in Bloom, ed., *The Brontës,* 72–73). Rosalind also remarks that "extremes lent themselves readily to the presentation of her [Emily's] own intense and strongly-varied apprehension; extremes were her natural mode" (77).

25. Chitham, *A Life of Emily Brontë,* 80–81; Lyn Pykett, *Emily Brontë,* 1.

and window, presentiment and conviction. In *Jane Eyre,* it is that emblem of Charlotte Brontë's controlled if not restrained presentation of the supernatural, the garden, with its cultivated profusion of flowers, that at one point provides a setting for the supernaturally underwritten relations between Jane and Rochester. In *Wuthering Heights,* it is the wild, heathered, and pristine moor unattached to any dwelling, unbounded by fence or wall, that expanse between Thrushcross Grange and Wuthering Heights, between heaven and hell, that provides the space for Catherine and Heathcliff's spirits. Unlike the houses and gardens of civilization and materiality, the moor and the crag remain unappropriable scapes not only of physical but also of natural and spiritual freedom.

The use of mirror and window by Charlotte and Emily Brontë, much like their employment of garden and moor in their texts, also characterizes their supernaturalism. When Jane Eyre looks into the mirror she ultimately recognizes in herself the ghost "specking the gloom" (*Eyre,* 11). When Catherine peers into the looking glass she cannot recognize herself; she is unable either to identify with or to claim her own reflection. Whereas Jane sees her own ghost, Catherine is bewildered and haunted by her antithesis, her doppelgänger.[26]

> "Who is it? I hope it will not come out when you are gone! Oh! Nelly, the room is haunted! I'm afraid of being alone!" . . .
>
> "There's nobody here!" I insisted. "It was *yourself,* Mrs. Linton; you knew it a while since."
>
> "Myself," she gasped, "and the clock is striking twelve! It's true, then; that's dreadful!" (*Heights,* 106)

As the clock strikes the witching hour, Catherine glimpses the horror of her own self-imposed loneliness. The thing that haunts her from the mirror is the opposite of Catherine Earnshaw. It is Catherine Linton, the being whose desire for standing in the visible and material world now stands between her and her "holy ghost," Heathcliff. She can reclaim that holy and truer self only by becoming a ghost. Although the distinction is a fine one, whereas Charlotte Brontë's mirror gives back the immateriality of a true self, Emily Brontë's gives back the

---

26. For discussions of doubling, dividing, and splitting in *Wuthering Heights,* see Anita Levy's *Other Women: The Writing of Class, Race, and Gender, 1832–1898,* 75–97. See also Bronfen, *Over Her Dead Body,* 305–13.

alienating materiality of a self her character longs to escape. Emily's Catherine has become, as Anita Levy has it, "the Victorian woman who embodies not only the self, the woman who is culturally acceptable, but also the other, the woman who is both the authentic object of desire and the one whom it is forbidden to desire."[27] In Emily's novel the "real" ghost is not reflected in the looking glass, it appears just beyond the window that overlooks the moors. In *Jane Eyre* the supernatural has the feel of a presentiment; in *Wuthering Heights* it packs the force of a conviction. Whereas supernaturalism in Charlotte Brontë's novel constitutes an opening up of spaces for the manifestation and liberation of deeper realities in the life of the oppressed female, in Emily Brontë's book the supernatural is ultimately the sole venue to power, possession, freedom, and self.

Ghosts have a place in the relations between Catherine and Heathcliff from the beginning and become more prominent as those relations are threatened with disintegration. One of the childhood pastimes of Catherine and Heathcliff is calling out the ghosts near Gimmerton Kirk: "We've braved its ghosts often together, and dared each other to stand among the graves and ask them to come" (*Heights*, 108). As innocent as it seems, this childhood game, which so impressed Catherine that she recalls it on her deathbed, prefigures the adult Catherine and Heathcliff's fervent if indeed not feverish insistence that the ghosts in themselves come out and come in. In fact, when Catherine is, on the one hand, violently pulled quite literally by her foot from the moor—the site, it is implied, of Heathcliff's mysterious origin—into the respectable material world of the Lintons, and when she, on the other hand, is pushed there by her brother Hindley's wife's "plan of reform" (*Heights*, 50), Catherine and Heathcliff experience a disruption of their united being that ultimately sets them on the path to spirit possession. Both Catherine, who early reaches out and seizes Linton and the trappings of wealth and respectability, and Heathcliff, who later gains a fortune and both the properties of the Heights and the Grange by holding on to bodies (his own and those of the properties' heirs) and houses, eventually learn that

27. Levy, *Other Women*, 89. Irene Tayler uses the term *holy ghosts* when she contends that "each of the Brontë sisters created a male muse, a Holy Ghost—one that was partly . . . the gender-reversed female muse of their male Romantic predecessors" (*Holy Ghosts: The Male Muses of Emily and Charlotte Brontë*, vii).

such essays at material possession are finally not as satisfying as they anticipated, surely not as fulfilling as spiritual possession will be.

As Nelly tells it, Catherine and Heathcliff spend many years dissolving each other, fretting away one another's flesh, calling each other into ghosts, as it were. On one level, Catherine proves the leader if not the controller in this fitful and painful dissolution into ghosthood. She unwittingly torments Heathcliff with her announcement to Nelly that she will marry Linton; then when the scorned Heathcliff returns after a three-year absence and she finds that neither Linton nor Heathcliff will do her bidding, she deliberately starves herself to death, again torturing Heathcliff more than Edgar, who recovers nicely from Catherine's willful death, being after all "too good to be thoroughly unhappy long. *He* didn't pray for Catherine's soul to haunt him" (*Heights,* 151). Heathcliff, as well as Catherine, sees that the way back to edenic union, the only way for them to repossess each other, is through ghosthood, a ghosthood in which the lovers "must remain located in between, in the transgressive and liminal position of the ghost."[28]

Heathcliff, in words that anticipate Tennyson's cry in *In Memoriam* (1850) that the spirit of his dead friend Hallam "Be near" him, prays similarly that Catherine become a spirit and volunteers to serve as the theater of her supernatural existence: "haunt me, then! . . . I know that ghosts *have* wandered on earth. Be with me always—take any form— drive me mad! only *do* not leave me in this abyss, where I cannot find you! Oh, God! it is unutterable! I *cannot* live without my life! I *cannot* live without my soul!" (*Heights,* 139). With his "strong faith in ghosts" and his conviction "that they can, and do exist, among us" (*Heights,* 229), Heathcliff is the only one in the novel who not only expects Catherine's return but also for some eighteen years feels her presence as the brink of his completion. After all, Catherine's return will constitute what Auerbach would call her "truer" self. "Nelly, I *am* Heathcliff—he's always, always in my mind—not as a pleasure, any more

---

28. Bronfen, *Over Her Dead Body,* 310. In her reading of *Wuthering Heights,* Bronfen also focuses on the novel's ghosts, or what she calls its revenants, a word that finally emphasizes the idea of the return more than it does liminality. In Bronfen's work, in which the revenant is presented in mainly psychoanalytic terms of the uncanny and the alter ego, the ghost ends up being one of several registers of the central subject of the text—death, or more specifically, the "interrelation between death, femininity and aesthetisation" (40).

than I am a pleasure to myself—but as my own being—so, don't talk of our separation again" (*Heights*, 74). Even as a spirit, Catherine confirms this idea that pleasure is not the mainstay of her being in Heathcliff. Their relation suggests that pain, which takes the measure of the soul, testing its stamina and suggesting its capacity for faith and for fusion, is the tie that really binds. Pain is what the specter of Catherine exacts from Heathcliff, who agonizes with no little satisfaction, "She showed herself, as she often was in life, a devil to me! And, since then, sometimes more, and sometimes less, I've been the sport of that intolerable torture! Infernal—keeping my nerves at such a stretch, that, if they had not resembled catgut, they would, long ago, have relaxed to the feebleness of Linton's" (*Heights*, 230).

Heathcliff, who has contributed to Catherine's escape into ghosthood by stripping and ruining Hindley and marrying Edgar's sister Isabel, not only invites Catherine to haunt him ("You said I killed you—haunt me, then! The murdered *do* haunt their murderers, I believe" [*Heights*, 139]) but also haunts her even after she has passed on. With spade in hand, Heathcliff makes his own ghoulish visitation to Catherine's grave; he scrapes at her coffin until she is roused to sigh and breathe her warm breath upon him (*Heights*, 228–29). Repeatedly over the twenty years after her death Heathcliff haunts the ghost, calling for it not only at the graveyard but also on the moors and in the bedchamber (*Heights*, 230).

It is in this last place, the room in the house associated among other things with privacy, repose, and sexual possession or union, that the specter of Catherine deals Heathcliff a painful rap by appearing "with a spectre's ordinary caprice" not to Heathcliff but to his tenant Lockwood, who comprehends nothing of his landlord's wretched need to be haunted. As far as Lockwood is concerned, Heathcliff's calling out of Catherine's ghost is superstitious nonsense and ridiculous folly (*Heights*, 33). But Heathcliff, who pleads, "Come in! come in! . . . Cathy, do come. Oh, do—*once* more! Oh! my heart's darling, hear me *this* time—Catherine, at last" (*Heights*, 33), aches with the desire that the gifts of the bedchamber—the peace, union, and the self he has known in that room with its oak-paneled bed—be his once more. It no doubt exasperates Heathcliff that the bumbling and blind Lockwood has invaded the sanctum of Cathy's bedchamber and experienced a revelation of her spirit that Heathcliff covets for himself. Indeed, Lockwood himself is not insensitive to the fact that not only by sleeping in the room, but also by reading Catherine's writings, he has intruded upon a private place and private feeling. His skeptical sneer at Heathcliff's passionate cry for the ghost's return is weighted with the shame and guilt of his violation of the intimate space and moment as well as perhaps a passing suspicion that the ghost of Catherine really has visited him: "I drew off, half angry to have listened at all, and vexed at having related my ridiculous nightmare [to Heathcliff], since it produced that agony, though *why*, was beyond my comprehension" (*Heights*, 33).

Lockwood's inability to comprehend is not a rarity in this novel. He does not comprehend love, so he runs from a woman in the city who pays him some attention. He does not understand Heathcliff, so he mistakenly assumes that he has much in common with his surly host. Most significant, he does not fully comprehend those supernatural imprints—his dreams—which finally provide as much insight into Catherine's predicament as into Lockwood's. Lockwood's first dream of accompanying Joseph to a church service where he suffers not only a tedious sermon on sin but finally the blows of the pilgrim-staffed congregation pulls together much of what Lockwood has discovered in the brief time that he has occupied Catherine's old room at Wuthering Heights. Examining an old "Testament, in lean type" as well as some other volumes in which Catherine had inscribed her childhood commentary, Lockwood lights upon a "caricature of . . . Joseph" and an account of an "awful Sunday" during which young Catherine and Heathcliff, "groaning and shivering" (*Heights*, 26) with cold as they are forced to endure Joseph's three-hour religious service, rebel. Lockwood reads about the children's oppression, rebellion, and punishment, then grows drowsy even as his eye catches "a red ornamented title—'Seventy Times Seven, and the First of the Seventy-First. A Pious Discourse delivered by the Reverend Jabes Branderham, in the Chapel of Gimmerden Sough.'" He falls asleep and dreams of oppression, defiance, and blows about his ears reminiscent of the ones that made Catherine write, "How little did I dream that Hindley would ever make me cry so. . . . My head aches, till I cannot keep it on the pillow" (*Heights*, 28, 27). Even as the dream eerily resurrects, if not Catherine herself, then Catherine's experience, it speaks to Lockwood's experience as well.

One of the most remarkable and amusing incidents in the first dream is Lockwood's effort to keep himself awake and conscious during the dream-sermon: "Oh, how weary I grew. How I writhed, and yawned, and nodded, and revived! How I pinched and pricked myself, and rubbed my eyes, and stood up, and sat down again, and nudged Joseph to inform me if he would *ever* have done!" (*Heights*, 29). The extreme discomfort Lockwood portrays here not only recalls the difficulty the children Catherine and Heathcliff must have had as they stood through a three-hour service, it also reveals a certain restlessness in Lockwood and his personal need for spiritual revitalization. He has, after all, difficulty staying put and finding his space, as is demonstrated by his flight from the city to the country, and almost immediately his trek from Thrushcross Grange to Wuthering Heights without his pilgrim staff, that is to say, without calling card or invitation. It is fitting that having sinned the sin that no man or woman need pardon by transgressing against his lover, Lockwood arrives at the house, but more specifically is ushered to the room that has been enshrined as the chapel of Catherine and Heathcliff's unorthodox fellowship. As he investigates the relics and traces of Catherine's childhood, he is well on his way to being exposed to one of the most powerful instances of that which he has feared and rejected—love.

If one accepts, as some critics have, the notion that Lockwood, like "everyman" who denies love, is the sinner of the sin no man need pardon, then Lockwood's second so-called dream follows necessarily from the first, since it constitutes a moment in which Lockwood, so adept at locking others out, may if he chooses revive himself by admitting both physically and spiritually the female ghost whose "lamentable prayer" is to be let in (*Heights*, 30).

Fearing the ghost's display of love and fidelity just as much as he does the budding affections of the woman in the city, Lockwood, who wants to be free of this eerie exposure of the female's self, brutally saws the ghost's arm across the broken pane of glass, betraying what Branderham in the first dream calls his "human weakness" (*Heights*, 29) and what Edgar Shannon Jr. has shown to be his capacity for a violence that characterizes nearly every character in the novel.[29] Oddly enough, by rejecting and

29. "Lockwood's Dreams and the Exegesis of *Wuthering Heights*," in Vogler, ed., *Twentieth Century Interpretations of "Wuthering Heights,"* 106–7.

then denying Catherine's ghost, Lockwood rejects not only a figure that interests him strongly and immediately (*Heights*, 26) but also one with which he himself is interestingly if tenuously associated. Like the ghost, for instance, he has difficulty gaining access to the Heights; he vaguely realizes his own insubstantiality when he imagines how the life of the city dweller is a mere specter of the richer lives of those living in the country:

> They *do* live more in earnest, more in themselves, and less in surface change, and frivolous external things. I could fancy a love for life here almost possible; and I was a fixed unbeliever in any love of a year's standing. One state resembles setting a hungry man down to a single dish on which he may concentrate his entire appetite, and do it justice; the other introducing him to a table laid out by French cooks. He can perhaps extract as much enjoyment from the whole, but each part is a mere atom in his regard and remembrance. (*Heights*, 58)

Finally Lockwood inadvertently links himself to Catherine as he seeks to align himself socially and temperamentally to her other half, Heathcliff. Association with the specter never approaches identification, however, as Lockwood remains trapped in himself, locked into his fear of participating in his own love affair or sympathizing with the love that has ultimately raised the ghost outside his window. It is significant that as he reads, dreams, and wakes, Lockwood is scarcely aware of the importance of Catherine's love for Heathcliff.

Dreams, like love, may rattle Lockwood's brains, but they do not touch his soul. A devotee, as critics have pointed out, of the rational, material, and utilitarian world, Lockwood no more fathoms the significance of his dream and the visitation than he meaningfully "decypher[s] her [Catherine's] faded hieroglyphics" (*Heights*, 26). When he does show signs of realizing that the "frightful nightmare" is "proof" of something beyond the fact that "the place was haunted . . . swarming with ghosts and goblins," Lockwood as quickly dispels this insight, as he does the "glare of white letters [which had earlier] started from the dark, as vivid as spectres—the air swarm[ing] with Catherines," inscribing her ghostly being (*Heights*, 31, 25). Brushing aside the force, the power, and the significance of what has happened to him in the paneled room, Lockwood concludes that the dream of Branderham, but especially Catherine's visit, was simply an "impression . . . personified" by an imagination out of control (*Heights*, 32).

For the rational Lockwood, the supernatural is tantamount to a loss of control, while for Catherine the supernatural ultimately translates into force, power, and control. Unlike Lockwood, who makes little enough of his dream of exposure and excommunication, Catherine understands that her dreams have the power to redefine reality: "I've dreamt in my life dreams that have stayed with me ever after, and changed my ideas; they've gone through and through me, like wine through water, and altered the colour of my mind" (*Heights,* 72). Her personal dream of being excommunicated or expelled from heaven onto the moors not only prophesies her ultimate turn away from the conventional, ortho-dox, and material world as represented by Christianity and Gimmerton Kirk, by Edgar Linton and Thrushcross Grange, to the embracing of supernaturalism and Heathcliff and the moors, but also confirms not the rational and practical energies that draw her to the worldly offering of the Grange but rather the spiritual energies that propel her into the ghosthood that culminates her moorland being.

Indeed, for Catherine, who has as a child wished for the whip of control, power, and authority, the ghost may well be, as Nina Auerbach says of theatrical ghosts, a manifestation "of grandeur and supreme authority."[30] Certainly Catherine declares to the housekeeper that when she dies she will be altered so as to be stronger, more powerful, inacces-sible, and grander: "Nelly, you think you are better and more fortunate than I; in full health and strength. You are sorry for me—very soon that will be altered. I shall be sorry for *you.* I shall be incomparably beyond and above you all" (*Heights,* 134). While Nelly views such talk as the theatrics of a spoiled and headstrong young woman, Catherine's words clearly anticipate the ghostly translation that will result in the reclamation of a transcendental space and thereby self.

Like the speaker in Arnold's "Stanzas from the Grand Chartreuse," Catherine has wandered between worlds. The Heights and the Grange, heaven and hell, have been the poles of the oppression and sepa-ration she has weathered. But unlike the Arnoldian speaker whose

30. Auerbach, *Private Theatricals,* 18. Also relevant to Catherine's wish for the "whip" of control is Cynthia Russett's phrenological discussion in a chapter entitled "How to Tell the Girls from the Boys," in which she comments, "Women . . . felt philoprogenitiveness (love of young) much more intensely, so intensely indeed, that as children they selected dolls and cradles for their play in preference to the drums, horses, and whips beloved of little boys" (*Sexual Science,* 19).

suspension between two worlds makes his life painfully ineffectual, at best a shadow life, Catherine welcomes her disembodiment, only needing to pull Heathcliff with her into the world in between to complete her destiny. In the end, ghosthood enables both Catherine and Heathcliff to experience their wanderings on the moor not as an Arnoldian purgatory or wasteland but as a supernatural consummation of their love and being.

In *Wuthering Heights* ghosthood is anything but a condition of ambivalence or powerlessness. Its gifts of possession, power, and completion, however, remain unintelligible to those who need to decipher hieroglyphics, who find in the words of those who are different gibberish, who execrate as damned those who choose to make their own religion, who fear and therefore cannot imagine the unquiet slumber of the grave.

Both *Jane Eyre* and *Wuthering Heights,* stories of indomitable and passionate female figures who must contend with various forms of oppression, are also histories in which the female protagonists are the focus and subject of supernatural auras and phenomena. Although Charlotte and Emily Brontë's treatments of the supernatural are finally as different as the type and magnitude of oppression that each female protagonist suffers and the manner in which that oppression is resolved, in both cases the supernatural enabled the sisters to explore with transcendent force woman's ambivalent position in a world that denies or frustrates her need for the autonomy, power, and action that can usually translate into either a coveted visibility or an equally prized freedom. The supernatural also helped these two writers probe and manifest the nature of spirituality as they understood it, to present the deeper reality of feelings and energies that have been perceived as unwomanly, and to explore the dynamics of difference.

4

A Ghost in the Noontide
George Eliot's Lifting of the Veil

Celtic roots, isolation at Haworth parsonage, even "their un-usually protracted adolescence," as Derek Traversi has it,[1] may help to account on a psychobiographical level for the lurid imaginations of the romantic Brontë sisters and for their supernatural stories, but what of George Eliot's experiment with supernaturalism? How is it that Eliot, an agnostic and intellectual, a self-proclaimed realist noted for her novels about provincial life, about reform, about the middlemarch of progress—how is it that this woman, arguably more in touch with the world and Victorian society than the moor-bound Brontë sisters at Haworth parsonage, came to try her hand at the supernatural tale?

Of all the Victorian women who wrote supernatural stories, Eliot was the least likely to have done so. In an early-twentieth-century revaluation of Eliot, David Cecil, who did not find her a particularly original thinker, nonetheless pronounced her a rationalist incapable of looking at anything "without analysing and diagnosing," incapable of entertaining the supernatural. "She was," according to Cecil, "a thorough-going Victorian rationalist" who "was not religious: the progress of thought and discovery to her made it impossible to believe in the supernatural."

---

1. "The Brontë Sisters and *Wuthering Heights*," 50.

Certainly, among the writers considered here, hers was the distinction of "constructing novels" by which "she engaged in an active dialogue with contemporary scientific thought."[2] An avowed realist, a positivistic thinker convinced that science provided the conceptual mode not only for the material but also for the social and moral progress of men and women, Eliot was no ghost seer; however, the history of her involvement in the supernatural revival of the age, an involvement that culminated in the publication of *The Lifted Veil*, demonstrates that she was not blind to the spiritual implications of tensions between the known and the unknown, the seen and the unseen, the actual and the possible, dichotomies that comprise the salient features of a ghostly feminine paradigm.

Even as a young girl, Mary Ann Evans revealed her strong love of the numinous through her "puritanical" if not near fanatical religiosity. Although the rationalistic movement of the times, represented in the persons of such freethinking friends as the Brays and Hennells, eventually bore down on Mary Ann's evangelicalism and crushed her formal belief, the feeling that there was some great unknown remained with her. Caroline Bray herself had early witnessed her friend's willful search for the mysterious and her receptiveness to weird phenomena. She recounted the mesmeric experience Eliot underwent in 1844, the year before Harriet Martineau published her *Letters on Mesmerism:* "Mr. Rathbone invited 2 agreeable gentlemen to dine with us: both firm believers in mesmerism and clairvoyance, though one of them [William Hodgson] seemed much too shrewd to believe in anything else: he nearly succeeded in mesmerizing M.A. [Mary Ann] to the degree that she could not open her eyes, and begged him most piteously to do it for her, which he did immediately by passes."[3] Like Martineau and Charlotte Brontë, Mary Ann Evans also "underwent a personal experiment" and allowed herself to be mesmerized; what is more, according to Bray's account, she clearly responded.

2. Cecil, *Early Victorian Novelists: Essays in Revaluation,* 296, 302; Sally Shuttleworth, *George Eliot and Nineteenth-Century Science: The Make-Believe of a Beginning,* ix.

3. Caroline Hennell Bray, "Mrs. Charles Bray to Mrs. Christian Hennell," in Gordon S. Haight, ed., *The George Eliot Letters,* 1:180; hereafter cited parenthetically as *GEL.* Alan W. Bellringer describes young Mary Anne Evans's "increasingly puritanical" religious views in *George Eliot.* See also Gordon S. Haight, *George Eliot: A Biography,* 19–24.

Agnostic, intellectual, and analytical as she became, the mature George Eliot still retained her open-mindedness about mystery. Thus, thirty years after her mesmeric experience, still drawn toward the mystery of the supernatural, she turned up at a table-rapping séance held at the home of the Erasmus Darwins. Her attraction to the supernatural is even spottily revealed in her longer realistic works: in *Romola*, Savonarola and Fra Luca have uncanny visions; in *Adam Bede*, the female prophet-preacher Dinah Morris and the incident of the rapping willow branch that marks Thias Bede's death counter the pragmatism of Adam; and in *Daniel Deronda*, the ardent, if not rabid, evangelicalism of young Mary Evans that had testified to a deep-lying desire to be in touch with the transcendent becomes transformed into the wider, deeper consciousness of the character Mordecai, who wields strange powers of foreknowledge.

Mordecai's eerie visionary powers prove as feminine and attractive as the intuition Eliot would mention in letters to two friends. Although, as a great novelist, she revealed in *Deronda* both her practical and intellectual love of words and her appreciation of the effort involved in acquiring knowledge, she would always keep a place in her heart where she could entertain, as she had earlier, the mystery of communication. "When a sort of haziness comes over the mind making one feel weary of articulated or written signs of ideas," she wrote in 1841 to her friend and teacher Maria Lewis, "does not the notion of a less laborious mode of communication, of a perception approaching more nearly to intuition seem attractive?" (*GEL*, 1:107). Again near the end of that same year in a letter to Martha Jackson, Evans would wonder fleetingly about that unorthodox power typically attributed to women: "The labour of acquiring knowledge is, I grant, its own reward, but should you not like a little more intuition, or rather intuitive power, just to enable one to take a sort of seven-leagued-boot stride that would make up for girlish miseducation and girlish idleness?" (*GEL*, 1:123). Of course, she would much later test a version of these intuitive powers of perception, revealing most vividly, explicitly, and sustainedly a predilection for the mysterious in her supernatural tale *The Lifted Veil*, recorded by the narrator on August 20, 1850, but actually published in 1859 in the July issue of *Blackwood's Magazine*. In this short novel in which the psychic powers of a Shelleyan protagonist inform the story, George Eliot, to the disapprobation of some of her most avid readers, demonstrates, among other things, the "soul's need of something hidden and uncertain for the maintenance of that doubt and hope and effort which are the breath of its life."[4]

During her literary career Eliot would publish her share of what Felicia Bonaparte, in her study of Eliot's poetic imagination, calls "misguided books." *The Lifted Veil*, which Bonaparte in fact never mentions, may seem deserving of a place among these works characterized by "mystery," "uncertain form," and "dubious perspective." Certainly publisher and critic alike did not quite know what to make of this history of the young man Latimer, who, already isolated by his retiring, feminine, and poetic nature from his hard-nosed banker father and his robust and selfish brother, Alfred, becomes positively alienated from his family, his friends, and the love of his life, Bertha Grant, when he develops clairvoyant powers of sight and sound. Eliot's apparent abandonment of reason and her turn to the supernatural in *The Lifted Veil* contributed to the perception of the work as an anomaly. Although readers of the story admit that it is, in the words of both George Henry Lewis and publisher John Blackwood, a "striking" and an "original" story, readers then and now have used such expressions as "painful," "woefully somber," "experimental," "strange," "disagreeable," "the weirdest fiction she ever wrote," and "aberration" to describe Eliot's tale. In 1968, U. C. Knoepflmacher, whose *George Eliot's Early Novels* includes one of the few sustained and insightful studies of *The Lifted Veil*, commented that "most students of George Eliot have dismissed 'The Lifted Veil' contemptuously as being 'mixed up with too much "spook stuff" to make the piece of more than passing interest.'" In the landmark *Madwoman in the Attic*, Sandra M. Gilbert and Susan Gubar declared, "While we are familiar with George Eliot's sympathetic concern for humanity, her historical representation of English country life, her critique of egoism, and her heroines' fascination with self-sacrifice, we are hardly prepared to have from her a story of gothic secrets, extrasensory powers of perception, and scientific experiments in revivification, all placed in an exotic Continental setting." Finally, B. M. Gray, in the fine "Pseudosciences and George Eliot's 'The Lifted Veil,'" observed, "'The Lifted Veil' seems to arouse embarrassment rather than interest, as if there were a general wish either that it had not been written

4. *The Lifted Veil*, 43; hereafter cited parenthetically as *Veil*.

at all or that it had been written by someone more appropriate—Poe . . . or Dickens."[5]

Interestingly enough, Eliot's feelings about the story were ambivalent. She introduced the story to Blackwood in a way that ultimately belies her concern for her "hideous progeny": "I have a slight story of outré kind—not a *jeu d'esprit,* but a *jeu de melancholie,* which I could send you in a few days for your acceptance or rejection as a brief magazine story—of one number only. I think nothing of it, but my private critic [George Henry Lewes] says it is very striking and original, and on the strength of that opinion, I mention it" (*GEL,* 3:41). Her casual reference to the story reads like a defense, in which she anticipates her publisher's and her readers' unenthusiastic response to its oddity. In her rather flippant extenuation of the tale to Blackwood, she undercuts her "brief magazine story," characterizing it as "slight," "outré," a piece that is little more than an insignificant bit of literary fluff that she happened to compose at a time when her "head was too stupid for more important work" (*GEL,* 3:60, n. 1). Even her use of terms like "outré," "*jeu de melancholie,*" and "schauderhaft"—quoted by her friend Edith Simcox, a social reformer who idolized Eliot (*GEL,* 9:220)—suggests ambivalence, at once both the allure and dignity as well as the distance and "otherness" that foreign terms can confer. The passing of time did even more to point up Eliot's inconsistent presentation of the story; whereas in 1859 she wrote, "I think nothing of it," by 1873, writing in response to Blackwood's request to republish the tale, she not only added an epigraph to help indicate the story's meaning but also admitted, "I care for the idea which it embodies and which justifies its painfulness" (*GEL,* 5:380). Still, as Mary Jacobus points out, "Eliot did not [publicly] acknowledge the story as hers until near the end of her life, in the Cabinet edition of 1877, and its anonymity dissociates it still further from the culturally

---

5. Bonaparte, *The Triptych and the Cross: The Central Myths of George Eliot's Poetic Imagination,* 1. In *George Eliot,* Haight wrote, "This experimental study of the stream of consciousness, with time sequence shifting to both past and future in a mode that Virginia Woolf was to develop, gives 'The Lifted Veil' a curiously modern quality. Except for *Theophrastus Such* it is the only one of George Eliot's narratives in the first person" (296). See Beryl Gray's afterword to *The Lifted Veil,* 69–70. Also see *GEL,* 9:220, where Edith Simcox, a young devotee and friend of Eliot's, writing in 1878 about a visit she paid to Eliot and George Henry Lewes, recalls her reaction to *The Lifted Veil:* "He asked what I thought of it. I was embarrassed and said—as he did—that it was not at all like her other writings, wherefrom she differed." Knoepflmacher, *George Eliot's Early Novels: The Limits of Realism,* 130; Gilbert and Gubar, *The Madwoman in the Attic: The Woman Writer and the Nineteenth-Century Literary Imagination,* 445; Gray, "Pseudoscience and George Eliot's 'The Lifted Veil,' " 408.

integrated George Eliot of the successful 'realist' novels, whether pastoral or European."[6]

Eliot conceived this spooky narrative in a period of considerable stress. She was just making the transition in selfhood from the unacknowledged Mary Ann Evans to the promising new writer George Eliot. Her *Scenes of Clerical Life* (1857) had stirred literary critics, and *Adam Bede* (1859) was a public success. She had recently revealed her identity to her publisher, John Blackwood, and now the time was approaching when the public too would pierce her pseudonym. In the final years of this decade, Eliot also, no doubt, felt even more severed from her family. Her brother, who had renounced personal dealings with her in 1854, remained alienated; her sister became ill and died. The supernatural *Lifted Veil* clearly reflects the pressures that beset the female writer and the isolation that this woman with the "massive" mind experienced.[7] Eliot would not have written such a story around the time of *Middlemarch,* when she was at the height of her successful writing career and could look back on almost two decades of G. H. Lewes's tried-and-true devotion.

Of the three adjectives that best characterize *The Lifted Veil*—*short, painful,* and *spooky*—the last is the most provocative and ultimately the most informative. The protagonist's weird powers account for much of what sets the story apart from the long, realistic novels we usually associate with George Eliot.[8] Henry James was one of the earliest commentators on the supernaturalism of the story, which he pronounced structurally and artistically quirky: he could not find a "connection between the clairvoyance of the hero and the [story's] incidents." More recently, Marghanita Laski, in her one brief mention of the story, concurs with the idea of a problematic supernaturalism, criticizing *The Lifted Veil* as "a sadly poor supernatural story." Whether the supernaturalism of the tale is as inexpedient as these two critics suggest, the fact is that

---

6. The phrase *hideous progeny* is taken from Mary Shelley's introduction to *Frankenstein.* For interesting parallels between *The Lifted Veil* and *Frankenstein,* see Knoepflmacher's *George Eliot's Early Novels,* chap. 5. Gilbert and Gubar also consider George Eliot's debt to Mary Shelley in *Madwoman in the Attic,* 455–57. Jacobus, *Reading Woman: Essays in Feminist Criticism,* 255.

7. Cecil, *Early Victorian Novelists,* 286.

8. In the afterword to *The Lifted Veil,* Gray suggests, to the contrary, that "painful" is the key word, that while "it is true that George Eliot's *treatment* of her idea is a departure for her," what "she wishes to justify [is] the story's painfulness, not its unorthodoxy." I would argue that one ought not separate treatment from the "idea itself" (72). It is significant that the idea of the pain George Eliot was trying to express could only be artistically conveyed through the supernatural.

Eliot's turn to the supernatural in the "miniaturized" novel was not only the inevitable expression of a woman and a writer in tune with the times but also and more specifically the expression of a dissonance she experienced as a woman in a society where too often the energies that begot recognition, acclaim, and material progress did so to the exclusion of energies that knitted lives together.[9]

Having its roots in the repudiation of Evangelicalism and having its most striking literary flowering in *The Lifted Veil*, which "bring[s] into focus," as B. M. Gray has noted, "George Eliot's comparatively unexplored interest in mesmerism . . . and clairvoyance," Eliot's involvement in Victorian supernaturalism has a significant budding in her work as behind-the-scenes editor of John Chapman's *Westminster Review*. In their mission (as Eliot herself finally construed it in the journal's 1852 prospectus) to recognize through contributions of the leading scientists and thinkers of the day "the Law of Progress," to "maintain a steady comparison of the actual with the possible," and to treat "controverted questions," the editors of the *Review* found themselves addressing the issue of pseudoscientific enthusiasms. For among the subjects that concerned and interested contributors such as Martineau and the Scottish phrenologist George Combe were not only Christian ethics, literature, physiology, and prison reform but also phrenology and the mesmerism that, as Howard Kerr has said of spiritualism in the United States, "probably helped stimulate the general appetite for supernatural fiction."[10] While it is true that not one of the articles published in the *Review* from 1852 to 1854, the dates of Eliot's unacknowledged editorship, treats phrenology or mesmerism per se, correspondence conducted on behalf of the *Review* is not barren of these subjects.[11]

In fact, early in George Eliot's career at the *Review*, the sticky issue of the phrenological and mesmeric movements presented itself when Combe, whose writings had converted Eliot's longtime friend Charles

9. James, " 'The Lifted Veil' and 'Brother Jacob,' " in Gordon S. Haight, ed., *A Century of George Eliot Criticism*, 131; Laski, *George Eliot and Her World*, 71; Harold Orel uses the phrase *miniaturized novels* in *The Victorian Short Story: Development and Triumph of a Literary Genre*, 61.

10. Gray, "Pseudoscience," 410; George Eliot, "Prospectus of the *Westminster and Foreign Quarterly Review*," 4, 5; Kerr, *Mediums, and Spirit-Rappers, and Roaring Radicals*, 55.

11. In fact, by May 1851 Eliot was already working with Chapman on the prospectus for the *Review*. The first issue under the joint editorship of Eliot and Chapman would not appear until January 1852. Eliot chose to no longer edit the *Review* in December 1853.

Bray to phrenology, apparently expressed concern that the *Review* was "about to become a very staid and decorous journal, conducted with due regard to the prejudices of the time" (*GEL*, 8:38). John Chapman, suspecting that Martineau and "those who think with her, on mesmeric matters," had probably instigated the "rumour," assured Combe that "If she or Dr. Gregory or any *able writer* whom we could rely on as competent to the task, were to offer us a paper embodying the well ascertained result of magnetic investigators it would be welcome, and if we distrusted the impartiality of the observer, his statements could be published in the 'Independent Section.'" Although Chapman aimed for open-mindedness, his concluding remarks about the phenomena make it clear that they are "questionable" subjects, "topics not yet within the domain of science" (*GEL*, 8:38, 39).

Eliot, who had first met Combe at the home of her good friend Charles Bray, wrote Combe herself three days later to defend the journal against the "imputation of 'trimming' and cowardice" and to second Chapman's statement about the *Review*'s position on mesmerism and phrenology. "The assertion that 'it [the *Review*] will not admit even an incidental allusion, if respectful, to such subjects as Mesmerism and Phrenology and that it ignores them altogether as topics of human thought and scientific investigation' is false," she declared. However, she hastened to add, being all the while careful to single out mesmerism, not phrenology, "But I think you will agree with me that the great majority of 'investigators' of mesmerism are anything but 'scientific'" (*GEL*, 8:41). Of the two would-be sciences—mesmerism, championed by Martineau, who occasionally contributed to the *Review*, and phrenology, which Combe practiced—phrenology received the gentler treatment from the *Review*'s editors. Both Chapman and Eliot were very careful about references to phrenology. On October 6, 1853, Chapman wrote a letter to placate Combe, who had proposed an article in which phrenology figured substantially:

> Dr. Hodgson was quite uninfluenced respecting the treatment of his article, and no word has passed between us as to the propriety of recognizing phrenology in his paper. No considerations of policy influence me in the least in determining how the Science of Phrenology shall be regarded by the *Westminster*. If my mind were clearly made up as to the possibility of applying *practically with success* the doctrine of

> phrenology to prison discipline the review should immediately endorse
> the recommendation of the system. (*GEL*, 8:80)

Again Chapman adroitly steered clear of the rocks of phrenology, re-
fusing to embrace the border science while managing to keep on good
terms with Combe.

Eliot also obviously wanted to maintain not just her professional but
also her personal relations with her friend George Combe and his wife,
both of whom she had met in 1851 at the home of the Brays; however,
it was not just her friendship with Combe but also her own experience
of phrenology that left her initially more receptive to it. Eliot had been
introduced to phrenology by Bray, who commented in his autobiography, "Mesmerism and Spiritualism, and their allied occult subjects, have
always had a special interest for me." While mesmerism and spiritualism,
the latter to which he finally objected, were special interests of Bray's,
phrenology became his real passion, and he devoted nearly fifty years of
his life to its study. It was Bray who in 1841 accompanied Marian Evans,
as she was now calling herself, to Deville's shop in the Strand, where she
had a cast taken of her then impressive twenty-two-and-a-quarter-inch
head. Forty years later Bray recalled, "George Combe, on first seeing the
cast [which Bray kept in his possession], took it for a man's."[12] Like Bray,
Combe must also have communicated his respect for the shape and size
of Marian's head, which he found as impressive as her accomplishments:

> Miss Evans is the most extraordinary person of the party. She translated
> Strauss's work "Das Leben Jesu" from the German, including the He-
> brew, Greek, and Latin quotations in it, without assistance; and it is said
> to be admirably executed. She has a very large brain, the anterior lobe is
> remarkable for length, breadth, and height, the coronal region is large,
> the front rather predominating; the base is broad at Destruc[tiveness];
> but moderate at Aliment[iveness], and the portion behind the ear
> is rather small in the regions of Comb[ativeness] Amat[iveness] and
> Philopro[genitiveness]. Love of approb[ation], and Concentrativeness
> are large. Her temper[ament] is nervous lymphatic. (*GEL*, 8:27)

12. Bray, *Phases of Opinion and Experience during a Long Life: An Autobiography*, 107, 74. See
also *GEL*, 1:167, for Mary Ann Evans's playful letter to Caroline Bray: "So you are going to have
Mr. Donovan and I shall miss my lessons from the arch-phrenologist! Never mind, I shall miss,
too, being told that I have some very bad propensities and that my moral and animal regions are
unfortunately balanced, all which is too true to be heard with calmness." On p. 193 of the same
volume, Haight, who also refers to Evans's letter to Bray on p. 51 of *George Eliot: A Biography*, notes,
"Cornelius Donovan gave Bray and GE a lesson in phrenology 22 February 1844."

While the influence and the appreciation of men and thinkers like Combe and Bray no doubt contributed to Eliot's willingness to entertain phrenology, the fact is that like many other Victorians she simply by her own lights found phrenology to be less mysterious, less haunted, than mesmeric phenomena. In a very fine article that uses Eliot's early experiences with phrenology to trace the influence of the pseudoscience on her "view of psychology," N. N. Feltes argues that what set phrenology apart from mesmerism in the mind of Eliot and others was its insistence on "the physical basis of mind." Karen Chase in her insightful study of the literary psychology of Charlotte Brontë, Dickens, and Eliot more precisely describes the difference between phrenology and mesmerism, observing that

> in many respects, the two doctrines made an unlikely alliance, sharing little more than their hostility to established psychological theories. Gall's phrenology stressed a physiological understanding of the mind; the brain was the site of human character . . . the structure of personality derived from anatomical structure. Mesmerism, on the other hand, with its hypothesis of a universal fluid and a complex system of attractions and repulsions, placed great emphasis on extra-individual forces.

In a general but more fitting statement for the purposes of this study, Feltes sums up the relation of a physically based phrenology to a mesmerism of "extra-individual forces": "Phrenology was . . . a bridge from the supernatural to the positive stage in psychology." Succinctly put, phrenology bypassed the supernatural. Years later when Marian Evans, editor for the *Westminster Review,* had become both George Eliot the novelist and Mrs. Lewes, the unofficial wife of George Henry Lewes, she would, as Feltes points out, reject "the clumsy systems of phrenology or physiognomy," dispensing with the " 'language' of phrenology," but keeping the " 'alphabet.' "[13]

Eliot's rejection of mesmerism and spiritualism proved more prompt and decisive than that of phrenology. As she indicated in two of her letters to Combe, mesmerism, or at least the people investigating it, was not "scientific":

13. Feltes, "Phrenology: From Lewes to George Eliot"; Chase, *Eros and Psyche,* 105–6; Feltes, "Phrenology," 15, 19, 21. Lewes probably influenced Eliot's rejection of phrenology. See Gray's "Pseudoscience" and Purkis's *Preface to George Eliot,* 37.

> We get impatient of phenomena which do not link on to our previous
> knowledge, and of which the laws are so latent as to forbid even the
> formation of a hypothesis concerning them. This and the great mass
> of loose statement and credulity which surround the whole subject of
> mesmerism repel many minds from it which are anything but bigoted
> or unenlightened. But indications of claire-voyance witnessed by a
> competent observer are of thrilling interest and give me a restless desire
> to get at more extensive and satisfactory evidence. (*GEL*, 8:45)

Although she herself had experienced something akin to a mesmeric
trance in 1844, Eliot would continue to feel that the laws of mesmerism
were too far removed from what she called in an essay on eighteenth-
century English poet and playwright Edward Young "the present and the
visible."[14] Mesmerism was neither clearly nor tidily rooted in previous
knowledge and therefore lacked the detail, continuity, and progression
that would make it historically and scientifically plausible. She much
preferred developments based on, to borrow a phrase from her own
Lifted Veil, the "slow details of labour" to any "strange sudden madness"
(*Veil*, 17). Eliot found a disorganization if not sloppiness of conception
about mesmerism that coupled with its mass appeal rendered it all but
untenable to the more discriminating mind.

Spiritualism she scorned outright, agreeing with Lewes that it was
a "monstrous folly of Table-turning and Spirit-rapping, which has revived," and with Bray, who had experienced "all sorts of fool's tricks"
at the séance table.[15] In 1853, before she had gone off to Weimar,
Germany, with Lewes, she had written to Combe about Robert Owen
and spiritualism, "By the bye, have you seen his [Owen's] last Manifesto
à propos of the Spirit Rappings? I will enclose it for your and Mrs.
Combe's amusement—if indeed you do not think it rather a sad than a
laughing matter" (*GEL*, 8:74). Whether Eliot was reacting to spiritualism
itself or to Owen's presentation of it matters less than her association of
spiritualism with incompetence. Already spiritualism was shaping up for

---

14. "Worldliness and Other-Worldliness: The Poet Young," 385.

15. Lewes, in "Letter to John Blackwood, 25 August [1860]" (*GEL*, 3:335), wrote, "At present I am
preparing a paper of a more popular character—"Seeing is Believing" [published in the *Fortnightly
Review*]—with a view to make people understand the difference between a *fact* and an *inference*.
It is with especial reference to the monstrous folly of Table-turning and Spirit-rapping which has
revived—and which the 'Cornhill Mag.' has the immorality (I can call it nothing else) to assist by a
paper in its favor, although Thackeray does not *pretend* to believe it." Bray, *Phases of Opinion*, 112.

her as a subject simultaneously of amusement, stupidity, and sadness. She was astonished if not amused in 1856 to discover that the daughter of William and Mary Howitt has been "taken in." "Have you heard that Anna Mary Howitt, alas! has become a spirit medium?" she wrote to her good friend Sara Hennell. "There is still enough of this folly left to give a form to monomania. Better be occupied exclusively with the intestinal worms of tortoises than with that" (*GEL*, 2:267). For her part, this "odious trickery" (*GEL*, 3:359), as she termed it in yet another letter to Hennell, was not worthy of serious consideration.

Yet the times were such that not only did Lewes write on the topic, but Eliot too had her thoughtful moments about the matter. Her correspondence with Harriet Beecher Stowe, for instance, required Eliot to think perhaps more than she cared about spiritualism, as a letter to the author of *Uncle Tom's Cabin* demonstrates. She wrote tactfully to Stowe on March 4, 1872:

> I desire on all subjects to keep an open mind, but hitherto the various phenomena reported or attested in connexion with ideas of spirit-intercourse, "psychism" and so on, have come before me here in the painful form of the lowest charlatanerie. Take Mr. Hume [Daniel Dunglas Home] as an example of what I mean. I would not choose to enter a room where he held a séance. He is an object of moral disgust to me, and nothing of late reported by Mr. Crookes, Lord Lindsay, and the rest carries conviction to my mind that Mr. Hume is not simply an impostor whose professedly abnormal manifestations have varied their fashion in order to create a new market, just as if they were papier mâché wares or pommades for the idle rich. But apart from personal contact with people who get money by public exhibitions as mediums, or with semi-idiots such as those who make a court for a Mrs. Guppy or other feminine personage of that kind, I would not willingly place any barrier between my mind and any possible channel of truth affecting the human lot. (*GEL*, 5:253)

Several months later Eliot, pestered if not haunted by the question of spiritualism, again found herself writing more thoroughly and decidedly about the matter. Having received letters from both Harriet and her husband Calvin Stowe about their personal experiences of spirit communication, Eliot replied gently, firmly, and, considering the parameters of the letter, at length:

Perhaps I am inclined, under the influence of the facts, physiological and psychological, which have been gathered of late years, to give larger place to the interpretation of vision-seeing as *subjective* than the Professor [Calvin Stowe] would approve. It seems difficult to limit—at least to limit with any precision—the possibility of confounding sense by impressions, derived from inward conditions, with those which are directly dependent on external stimulus. In fact, the division between within and without in this sense seems to become every year a more subtle and bewildering problem.

Your experience with the *planchette* is amazing; but that the words which you found it to have written were dictated by the spirit of Charlotte Brontë is to me (whether rightly or not) so enormously improbable, that I could only accept it if every condition were laid bare, and every other explanation demonstrated to be impossible. (*GEL*, 5:280–81)

While Eliot was able to account rationally for Professor Stowe's "vision-seeing" as a confusion of internal with external conditions, as what she describes elsewhere in her comments on biblical criticism and spiritual existence as more likely to be "the hallucination of an intense personality than to have any foundation in reason" (*GEL*, 8:70), Harriet Stowe's spiritual intercourse with no less a figure than Charlotte Brontë proved so egregiously "amazing" and unopen to rational construction that Eliot finally admitted to Stowe, much as Huxley did to the Dialectic Society, that she could not be bothered with such hocus-pocus, having better things to do in the short time that remained:

If it were another spirit aping Charlotte Brontë—if here and there at rare spots and among people of a certain temperament, or even at many spots and among people of all temperaments, tricksy spirits are liable to rise as a sort of earth-bubbles and set furniture in movement, and tell things which we either know already or should be as well without knowing—I must frankly confess that I have but a feeble interest in these doings, feeling my life very short for the supreme and awful revelations of a more orderly and intelligible kind which I shall die with an imperfect knowledge of. If there were miserable spirits whom we could help—then I think we should pause and have patience with their trivial-mindedness; but otherwise I don't feel bound to study them more than I am bound to study the special follies of a particular phase of human society. Others, who feel differently, and are attracted towards this study, are making an experiment for us as to whether anything better than bewilderment can come of it. At present it seems to me that to rest any fundamental part of religion on such a basis is a melancholy misguidance of men's minds from the true sources of high and pure emotion. I am comforted to think that you partly agree with me here.

I have not time to write more than this very imperfect fragmentary sketch of *only one* aspect which the question of spirit-communications wears to me as [*sic*] present. (*GEL,* 5:280–81)

Suffice it to say that Eliot was herself "particularly sensitive to the repulsive aspects" of "the modern movements," namely mesmerism and spiritualism, which led "men's minds from the true sources of high and pure emotion" (*GEL,* 5:48), from the real and pressing issues in Victorian life and from the light of truth to the strange, to the unknown, and to an emotional, spiritual, and intellectual darkness.

Oddly enough, while Eliot set aside unhesitantly mesmerism and spiritualism, she was more receptive to the notion of clairvoyance, avowing that "indications of claire-voyance witnessed by a competent observer are of thrilling interest and give me a restless desire to get at more extensive and satisfactory evidence" (*GEL,* 8:45). She apparently dissociated clairvoyance from the suspect phenomena of mesmerism and spiritualism that others like Dr. John Elliotson and Catherine Crowe had found either part and parcel of each other or at least interconnected. Whereas mesmerism could tool Charlotte Brontë's exploration of the spirit of a strong-willed woman, clairvoyance would inform Eliot's representation of an emotional and spiritual no-woman's land of in-betweenness.

Before turning to the story of Latimer in *The Lifted Veil,* it is appropriate to ask why Eliot separated clairvoyance from the other suspect occurrences. The answer lies mainly in her focus on and strong interest in seeing things clearly and whole and in hearing what she refers to in chapter 20 of *Middlemarch* as the roar on the other side of silence. Her novels are generously sprinkled with references to the senses of sight and sound, with references to a kind of clairvoyance and the clairaudience with which it often went hand in hand.[16] Subtle as they are, the spiritualized eye and ear, she indicates, can not only enhance but also be integral to our understanding of events, ourselves, and our world. Thus, in her Wordsworthian prelude to *The Mill on the Floss,* the chapter "Outside Dorlcote Mill," references to hearing—"deaf,"

16. C. W. Leadbeater, *Clairvoyance,* 1–2.

"dreamy deafness," "curtain of sound"—abound, while the chapter itself constitutes finally a seeing or reseeing with the mind's eye. This dreaming and remembering is effected through a narrative voice itself heard fitfully in this text about Maggie Tulliver's need not only to love and be loved but also to be seen and heard, to become, as it were, visible.

In *Daniel Deronda*, Eliot sets herself up as one who can see things in a drop of ink. She may here be numbered among what C. W. Leadbeater, writing at the end of the nineteenth century, described as "the largest and most widely-spread band of these semi-intentional clairvoyants . . . those who, as Mr. Andrew Lang puts it, 'stare into a crystal ball, a cup, a mirror, a blob of ink (Egypt and India), a drop of blood (among the Maories of New Zealand), a bowl of water (Red Indian), a pond (Roman and African), water in a glass bowl (in Fez), or almost any polished surface.'" Eliot even grants her creation Gwendolen Harleth underdeveloped powers of clairvoyance that finally go a good way toward redeeming her character. Her sighting of and reaction to the face in the cabinet inspire a "dread" that proves premonitory of her relations with the languid-unto-death husband, Grandcourt. More important, however, is the fact that Gwendolen's reaction to the eerie face in the cabinet affords readers a glimpse of her spirituality, her soul's vitality, and her ability to get beyond a spoiled self, a self whose ability to see clearly has been muddled and limited by egoism. *Daniel Deronda* formulates in interesting ways the theme prevalent in Eliot's work—the theme of seeing and hearing, so instrumental in "the future widening of knowledge" and thereby sympathy. In *Deronda* both the seerlike narrator and Gwendolen are imbued with a consciousness and with a conscience that, as Eliot writes of Deronda's, "included sensibilities beyond the common, enlarged by his early habit of thinking himself imaginatively into the experience of others," much as a clairvoyant transports himself or herself or is transported through time, space, or into the experience of others.[17]

In the larger realistic texts, *Daniel Deronda* and *Middlemarch,* in which Eliot is wont to direct a microscope on a drop of water, the surfacing of phenomena connected to and suggestive of clairvoyance demonstrates how Eliot could put aside the microscope and take up her crystal ball to

17. Ibid., 100; Eliot, *Daniel Deronda*, 50, 570.

gaze more deeply into the inner life. Eliot's visionary mission as a writer was to be true to what Bonaparte recognizes as "the sensibilities that concerned her, the deepest sensibilities, [which] are and must remain by their very nature inarticulate." Clairvoyance negotiated the plateau between the senses and those deep-lying sensibilities. It held out the possibility of an ability "to see much that is invisible to his fellow-men, and hear much that is inaudible to them." To her way of thinking and to that of some others, clairvoyance was not so very alien, or unconnected to established and accepted knowledge. People were not necessarily, to borrow Leadbeater's words about astral matter, required

> to imagine some new and strange kind of matter, but simply to think of the ordinary physical kind as subdivided so very much more finely and vibrating so very much more rapidly as to introduce us to what are practically entirely new conditions and qualities.
>
> It is not then difficult for us to grasp the possibility of a steady and progressive extension of our senses, so that both by sight and by hearing we may be able to appreciate vibrations far higher and far lower than those which are ordinarily recognized.

Clairvoyance was not about the unempirical ghosts and spirits of which Eliot's friend Charles Bray had written, "I reject the 'spirits' altogether. Spirits have been called in to account for every unknown cause ever since the world began. There are no greater wonders in Spiritualism than in Mesmerism, and we don't need spirits to account for thought-reading and clairvoyance."[18] Clairvoyance was about human potential, about the extension of our senses, about the possibility of knowing, communicating, feeling, and connecting.

In *The Lifted Veil,* neither the tutor's phrenological assessment of Latimer's head nor the scientist's spectacular revivification of the maid by blood transfusion is at the heart of the story. Latimer's clairvoyant powers are. While the story lends itself to Knoepflmacher's investigation of self-division, to Gilbert and Gubar's investigation, among other things, of "the myth of feminine evil," to Gray's study of "moral journey," or to Jacobus's Freudian exploration of hysterics and reminiscences, *The Lifted Veil* can more dynamically be read as a story about spirituality,

---

18. Bonaparte, *The Triptych and the Cross,* 77; Leadbeater, *Clairvoyance,* 9, 11; Bray, *Phases of Opinions,* 112.

specifically about the condition of one who, spiritually capable, operates in the "real" world, or as Gearhart would say, "In a world where every nook and cranny has been filled with superficialized and competitivized external energy."[19] Latimer's father, "in root and stem a banker," is committed to a life in which progress consists in securing and ensuring "county influence" and "aristocratic position" (*Veil*, 5, 6). Latimer's older brother, Alfred, a "perfect stranger" to Latimer, proves an irritating rival with the "superficial kindness of a good-humoured, self-satisfied nature, that fears no rivalry, and has encountered no contrarieties" (*Veil*, 20). When Latimer gains his powers of clairvoyance, the superficiality and egoism of such beings is painfully magnified to reveal "all the intermediate frivolities, all the suppressed egoism, all the struggling chaos of puerilities, meanness, vague capricious memories, and indolent make-shift thoughts, from which human words and deeds emerge like leaflets covering a fermenting heap" (*Veil*, 19–20).

Latimer's new powers do not make him feel more at home in the world he inhabits. His insights into the meanness and pettiness of those souls around him ultimately stymie any real chance of happiness through human fellowship. On the one hand, he cannot relate to or negotiate the nothingness that he finds in others; on the other hand, others, Latimer feels, will not tolerate his sibyl-like power to read their innermost being. Because the people around him have no rich spiritual depths, Latimer, fearing by now not just further alienation but hostile rejection, must maintain a surface or facade that will not betray his ability to discover their lack. As William Myers put it, "The real barrier between him and humanity is not his visionary experience, but his inability to endure the exposure of talking about it."[20] Where surface meets surface, as it does here, there is little chance for sympathy.

Unsurprisingly, there is little enough sympathy for Latimer not only in the story itself but also in the critical community, which has read him as an ungenerous, unprepossessing sort of character. Gilbert and Gubar, who in their shrewd analysis of *The Lifted Veil* variously describe Latimer

---

19. Knoepflmacher, *George Eliot's Early Novels;* Gilbert and Gubar, *Madwoman in the Attic,* 466; Gray, afterword to *The Lifted Veil,* 72; Jacobus, *Reading Woman,* 254–74; Gearhart, "Womanpower: Energy Re-Sourcement," in Spretnak, ed., *The Politics of Women's Spirituality,* 196.

20. Myers, *The Teaching of George Eliot,* 233. Gilbert and Gubar comment in *Madwoman in the Attic* that Latimer "can read others but . . . will determinedly hide his own subjectivity out of a sense of shame and fear of self-exposure" (475).

as "disagreeable," "misanthropic," a "self-indulgent, self-pitying poseur," and a misogynist, perhaps best demonstrate the objection to Latimer's character when they speculate that Bertha Grant may well have had good reason to detest Latimer, who must "represent to her the impoverishment of desire and the renunciation of vitality." What Latimer manifests in what other critics have identified as his complaints and whining is not only the difficulty of possessing and revealing "internally sourced" powers that do not always or necessarily translate into material gains, but also, and most especially, the difficulty of being trapped between two worlds, caught in the bind of what Latimer himself recognizes as "double consciousness" (*Veil*, 32, 55, 66).[21]

Latimer's clairvoyant powers position him between the wearying and chilly emptiness of the material and mechanical world of the father and the warmth, comfort, and richness of the spiritual and natural world of the mother. The horror for Latimer is that he cannot use his newly found powers to move forward in a world that, for all its vaunted respect for the poet, the priest, and the angel in the house, shows itself to be even more respectful of the scientist, the banker, and the heir. It is this second, more soul-affirming world that Latimer seeks to recapture. At a time when "the curtain of the future was as impenetrable to [him] as to other children," Latimer had "had a tender mother," and "unequalled love" that "soon vanished out of [his] life, and even to [his] childish consciousness it was as if that life had become more chill" (*Veil*, 4). Upon the death of his mother, Latimer becomes increasingly isolated and "hungry for human deeds and emotions" (*Veil*, 7). When the curtain of the future lifts, one of Latimer's most important moments of clear seeing consists in the vision and materialization of the "pale, fatal-eyed woman, with the green weeds . . . like a birth from some cold sedgy-stream, the daughter of an aged river" (*Veil*, 16). In words evocative not only of "La Belle Dame sans Merci" but also of Botticelli's Venus, Latimer bespeaks his urgent need to resurrect that unequaled love of the mother, to appease his hunger for human love and sympathy at the breast of this woman. Unfortunately, Bertha, Latimer discovers, is the opposite of his angelic, nurturing mother, "the very opposite, even to the colour of her hair, of the ideal woman who still remained to me

---

21. Gilbert and Gubar, *Madwoman in the Attic,* 447, 446, 461, 459, 461; see also Ruby V. Redinger, *George Eliot: The Emergent Self,* 401.

the type of loveliness . . . [Bertha] was [even] without that enthusiasm for the great and good" (*Veil*, 22). Latimer marries La Belle Dame sans Merci, a witch, his mother's doppelgänger.[22]

Before Latimer confirms Bertha's commitment to the world of egoism and superficiality, he enjoys the uncertainty and thereby the possibility of love. Because Latimer cannot see into the mind of Bertha the girl, she becomes "the fascination of an unravelled destiny," an "oasis of mystery in the dreary desert of knowledge," his La Gioconda (*Veil*, 21, 26). As impenetrable as Jane Eyre was to her Rochester, Bertha proves even more alluringly and refreshingly so to Latimer, but only for a while. Bertha the wife eventually realizes Latimer's prevision of her as the "cruel-eyed" Borgia woman whose "pitiless soul" is one of "barren worldliness" and "scorching hate" (*Veil*, 28, 29). When Latimer discovers that his wife has planned to poison him, he experiences what Barbara Starrett describes as "one of the hardest, most devastating shocks of the women's movement . . . to learn that women, too, can damage us, can drain us." If Latimer is not exactly drained, he is arrested because Bertha is not the conduit for more loving, peaceful, and creative energies. She proves, if not one of the purveyors of the material world, then the perversion of the sympathy and spiritual affirmation Latimer seeks. For she is certainly the castrating and cannibalistic woman Gilbert and Gubar and Jacobus identify, but even more provocatively she is, as Starrett would call her, one of the vampires who "seek power through other women, or else use their own power to flail with the weapons of negative emotion."[23] Indeed, Bertha reveals herself a vampire precisely at the moment that she anticipates the death of her maid, whom she planned to use to poison

22. Gilbert and Gubar mention not only Keats's "La Belle Dame sans Merci" but also "Goethe's *Faust*, Shelley's 'Medusa,'" and "all of Swinburne's various Ladies of Pain" in commentary on Bertha's relation to "the Romantics' fascination with the fatal female and the deathly principle she represents." They note, "Associated, as she is, with sirens, serpents, Eve, Cleopatra, Lucrezia Borgia, water-nixies, and sprites, Bertha is no less a representative of a popular type in the Romantic mythology of women than Maggie Tulliver, Rosamund Vincy, and Gwendolen Harleth—fatal females whose beauty, we shall see, is both sinister and tempting" (*Madwoman in the Attic*, 460); see also Jacobus's *Reading Woman*, in which she associates Bertha with "the death of desire," with "the enigma of woman which Freudian theory at once fails to unravel and unveils as castrating lack or absence" (268, 266).

23. Walter Pater fathoms Latimer's desire for Bertha as he describes Leonardo Da Vinci's masterpiece *La Gioconda* as "the presence that rose thus so strangely beside the waters . . . expressive of what in the ways of a thousand years men had come to desire" (*The Renaissance: Studies in Art and Poetry*, 124); Starrett, "The Metaphors of Power," in Spretnak, ed., *The Politics of Women's Spirituality*, 192; Gilbert and Gubar, *Madwoman in the Attic*, 465, 460; Jacobus, *Reading Woman*, 264–67.

Latimer: Bertha's "features at that moment seemed so preternaturally sharp, the eyes were so hard and eager—she looked like a cruel immortal, finding her spiritual feast in the agonies of a dying race" (*Veil,* 63).[24]

Unlike Bertha, who is best described as vampiric, Latimer is ghostly because his powers do not substantiate his being in the world of the father. Unable either to operate successfully in the material world or to return to the domestic comfort of the mother, Latimer is a ghost because he cannot "create new reality," because he is forever in between. Caught in what Jacobus terms a "purgatorial circularity" where "nothing is resolved, nothing renewed," Latimer can only "reinscribe" those "critical events of his own life and the date and manner of his death" because "writing is death." He cannot make a new world, he can only see the city of Prague, where, according to Gilbert and Gubar, "Creation is not possible . . . where Swift's Struldbrugs or Tennyson's Tithonus would be at home."[25]

It is fitting that Latimer's very first clairvoyant episode centers in Prague. This vision of the feminine city, which takes its name from the Czech words *Praha* and *Prah,* meaning "threshold," not only marks for Latimer both a beginning of new insights and the ending of old ignorances but also provides for the reader one of the strongest clues to the nature of Latimer's condition. Prague, which lies about two hundred miles from the better-known Vienna, has been described as a place in which "nothing is clear and simple . . . everything is enigmatic and complex," a mystical city held in time, "a living rudiment of the Middle Ages." Its cemeteries and synagogues, catacombs, Faust House, and statues of ecstatic saints all contribute to what some of the poets of Prague believed the "oppressive power of local mysticism." One Paul Cohen-Portheim, after visiting Prague, is reported to have written about "Hradčany [a castle] with its legends, the house where Dr. Faust lives, the whole atmosphere of magic and mystic, of the supernatural and mysteries that is stronger here than in any other city." By choosing "the mystical city" of Prague,[26] Eliot associates Latimer and his new powers

24. In *Madwoman in the Attic,* Gilbert and Gubar take exception to the idea that Bertha is a monster, arguing that behind the veil is no monster but a madwoman (472).

25. Starrett, "The Metaphors of Power," in Spretnak, ed., *The Politics of Women's Spirituality,* 193; Jacobus, *Reading Woman,* 259; Gilbert and Gubar, *Madwoman in the Attic,* 456.

26. Joseph Wechsberg, *Prague: The Mystical City,* 49, 53. See also Ernest Roth, *A Tale of Three Cities,* and Gustav Janouch, *Franz Kafka und seine Welt.* I am deeply indebted to Wechsberg's work, in which

with a mysterious supernaturalism that finally describes suspension and
arrestment:

> a city under the broad sunshine, that seemed to me as if it were the sum-
> mer sunshine of a long-past century arrested in its course—unrefreshed
> for ages by the dews of night, or the rushing rain-cloud; scorching the
> dusty, weary, time-eaten grandeur of a people doomed to live on in the
> stale repetition of memories, like deposed and superannuated kings
> in their regal gold-inwoven tatters. The city looked so thirsty that the
> broad river seemed to me a sheet of metal; and the blackened statues,
> as I passed under their blank gaze, along the unending bridge, with
> their ancient garments and their saintly crowns, seemed to me the
> real inhabitants and owners of this place, while the busy, trivial men
> and women, hurrying to and fro, were a swarm of ephemeral visitants
> infesting it for a day. It is such grim, stony beings as these, I thought,
> who are the fathers of ancient faded children, in those tanned time-
> fretted dwellings that crowd the steep before me; who pay their court
> in the worn and crumbling pomp of the palace which stretches its
> monotonous length on the height; who worship wearily in the stifling
> air of the churches, urged by no fear or hope, but compelled by their
> doom to be ever old and undying, to live on in the rigidity of habit, as
> they live on in perpetual mid-day, without the repose of night or the
> new birth of morning. (*Veil*, 11–12)

Inhabited by the extremes of men and women who swarm like
"ephemeral visitants infesting it for a day" and blackened statues with
their "blank gazes," "grim, stony figures" lined up along the bridge,
Prague holds under the glare of the broad sunshine flesh and stone,
living and dead, the soon to die and the dead who yet live, life-in-
death and death-in-life. It is a purgatorial city forever in between,
a city of "perpetual mid-day." "Strange," "unfamiliar," "a mere name,
with vaguely-remembered historical associations" (*Veil*, 12), Prague is as
ghostly as Latimer, whose story is a quintessential study of a ghostliness
that can provide a telling paradigm for the condition particularly of
the middle-class Victorian woman who found herself in a ghostlike

---

he lends strength to this idea of suspension and in-betweenness when he quotes one of "Prague's
German-writing poets," Willy Haas: " 'We were suspended in a vacuum—that was our own curse and
also our blessing,' remembers Willy Haas. 'Everybody had to think for himself, to start at the very
beginning, with the truth and the lie of our existence" (54–55). This language of suspension, curse
and blessing, truth and lie is very similar to that which ultimately characterizes George Eliot's stories
about her would-be poet, Latimer.

suspension between the blessing of pedestaled womanhood and the curse of a domestic confinement that vitiated her presence in the realm of banks, courts, and laboratories.

The Lifted Veil begins by highlighting the female phenomenon of waiting. As Elizabeth Gaskell's Margaret so aptly puts it in *Mary Barton* when she advises her girlfriend, the eponymous Mary, "Ay, dear: being patient is the hardest work we, any of us, have to go through life, I take it. Waiting is far more difficult than doing."[27] The first and last passages that frame *The Lifted Veil* are about waiting. Latimer waits for the heart failure and subsequent suffocation that he has already foreseen will take place on September 20, 1850. As he waits, he writes his life's history in such a way that it becomes evident that the internal powers he is granted are not ones that afford him more mobility or authority in the world but require that he suffer and be still, that he wait like Penelope. So Latimer waits for the realization of his clairvoyant perception of Prague. He waits for the transformation of Bertha from a flirtatious would-be sister-in-law into his own hateful and despising wife. Waiting, he begins "to taste something of the horror that belongs to the lot of a human being whose nature is not adjusted to simple human conditions" (*Veil*, 17), the horror, too, that belongs to those human beings whose natures are not just mysterious but sensitive and feminine. Again, like the ghost, his being is postponed.

Latimer's spectral condition of in-betweenness also manifests itself in his characterization as a medium of gender. "Held to have a sort of half-womanish, half-ghostly beauty" (*Veil*, 20), indeed "dogged," in the words of Jacobus, "by feeling like a girl," Latimer experiences an ambiguity of gender that renders him ineffectual in both the materialistic world of his punctual banker father and hearty brother and the Romantic world he wants to cohabit with Bertha. Passive, fainting, weak, but mentally and spiritually charged, Latimer suffers the double bind of the present-but-absent status associated with women and ghosts. Significantly, only Bertha is able to identify Latimer's womanish and ghostly powers. She recognizes in him the very mystery with which he has ardently sought to endow her; however, while he eagerly welcomes the mystery in Bertha, she contemns it in him. It would seem that the mystery and super-

27. Elizabeth Gaskell, *Mary Barton*, in *The Works of Mrs. Gaskell*, ed. A. W. Ward, 1:164.

natural aura that are granted to and even felt attractive in the female
are not acceptable in the male. Eliot ironically underscores the idea
by taking the erstwhile inscrutable female, Bertha Grant, masculinizing
her, then giving her a glimpse into the ghost seer.[28] "Keen, sarcas-
tic, unimaginative, prematurely cynical . . . critical and unmoved in the
most impressive scenes, inclined to dissect," Bertha comes to despise
Latimer as the real "energumen," if not angel in the house (*Veil*, 22,
27). Virile in her pragmatism, in her "tact and acuteness," her "*badinage
and playful superiority*," her "inaccessib[ility] to feminine agitations,"
Bertha recognizes in the "fragile, nervous," and "morbidly sensitive"
Latimer, "who made so poor a figure as an heir and a bridegroom,"
the pitiful powerlessness yet unnerving power of "a miserable ghost-
seer, surrounded by phantoms in the noon-day" (*Veil*, 45, 44, 59, 20,
22, 46, 48).

In *The Lifted Veil*, Eliot explores the dynamics of energies that are
not so much intellectual as emotional, social, and spiritual. Having been
briefly nurtured in the angelic love of his mother, Latimer grows into an
individual whose gifts have little to no real worth in the male-centered
materialistic world in which he lives; consequently, his feminine and
poetic energies are never fully or fruitfully realized: they remain as halved
as his womanish and ghostly beauty because they need the sympathetic
recognition of others to come fully into being and operation. To the
extent that Latimer's powers are realized, they leave Latimer suspended
between action and inaction, angel and demon, gift and curse. As a seer,
granted an unusual share of what Gilbert and Gubar have identified as
the domestic powers vouched the Victorian female to see into the soul
and needs of others, Latimer is unable to use these powers to "soften and
attract," to knit well the domestic circle.[29] The domestic and spiritual
knowledge with which he is blessed or cursed, the sympathy that is in
great part a clear seeing into the lives of others, makes him a ghost in
the noontide with all the ghost's potential to raise the consciousness,
but with all its ineffectiveness or compromised powers in the broad
light of day.

---

28. Jacobus, *Reading Woman*, 262; Jacobus identifies Bertha as "the woman who possesses the
fantasized phallus, the imaginary wholeness which endows her for Latimer with her mysterious
allure" (265–66).

29. *Madwoman in the Attic*, 449.

5

WOMAN WITCHED

THE SUPERNATURAL TALES OF ELIZABETH GASKELL

CHARLOTTE AND Emily Brontë's supernaturalism lends their works
an "excitement, interest, stimulus" of which readers and critics tend to
be in awe. The supernaturalism that informs George Eliot's *The Lifted
Veil* occasions some objection, even embarrassment; nevertheless, it
does make the story an interesting anomaly. The Brontës' and Eliot's
supernatural essays, though wondered at or marveled over either as
exceptional or as exceptions, are hardly excoriated. Yet the supernatural
stories of the friend and biographer of Charlotte Brontë, Elizabeth
Gaskell, tend all too often to be lumped into the damning category
of peripheral mishmash. Patsy Stoneman observes, "Irritation changes
to embarrassment when critics deal with Elizabeth Gaskell's minor
works, many of which have subjects—ghosts, bandits, witches, murders,
madmen, imprisonment, torture, mutilation—which 'fit' neither her
earnest social image nor her cosy feminine one. Many of these stories
have been out of print since 1906, and critics tend to dismiss them as
'fancies' . . . or 'melodrama.' "[1]

Yet those critics who have in Thomas Huxley's fashion declined to
listen to what may well sound to them like "The chatter of old women

---

1. See Shorter, *The Brontës*, 2:83; Stoneman, *Elizabeth Gaskell*, 8–9.

and curates in the nearest cathedral town" have shunted aside, especially in Gaskell's "The Old Nurse's Story," work finally much more representative than anything by the Brontës or Eliot of the Victorian ghost story. For as Cox and Gilbert note in opening the Oxford anthology of Victorian ghost stories with "The Old Nurse's Story," "Elizabeth Gaskell's 'The Old Nurse's Story', which dates from 1852, exhibits essential Victorian qualities—not least in its homely detail and disciplined treatment of supernatural events." Michael Ashley, in his introduction to *Mrs Gaskell's Tales of Mystery and Horror,* also asserts that "the place held by Mrs Gaskell in the development of the horror short story is undeniably a focal point" and that "she was able to disseminate through her work all that had been established in the genre since the publication in the preceding century of the first Gothic novel. . . . Writers thereafter took their cue from her and developed a specially puritan form of horror story, which became almost exclusively the domain of the woman writer." In his biographical introduction to *The Works of Mrs. Gaskell,* A. W. Ward describes Gaskell as a practical Victorian irresistibly drawn to ghosts. "Though reasonableness and a lucidity of mind which mirrored itself in a style of perfect clearness were among her most unfailing characteristics as a writer, yet her imagination was unmistakably attracted by whatever bordered on, or partook of, the supernatural." Elsewhere Ward remarks that Gaskell's "inclination to allow her mind to hover on the borders of the supernatural" was one "in which, like many persons of excellent sense, she occasionally indulged."[2] Like Charlotte Brontë's *Jane Eyre,* which uses the supernatural to explore and express difference and oppression, Emily Brontë's *Wuthering Heights,* with its emancipatory supernaturalism, and George Eliot's *Lifted Veil,* wherein the supernatural lends itself to an investigation of the spaces and tensions between the actual and the possible, the material and the spiritual, Gaskell's short stories afford further insight into the uses to which a woman writer could put the supernatural.

More than Charlotte Brontë, so long shut up at Haworth parsonage, but finally, after the success of her novel, making an excursion into "this big Babylon," as she called London, more so even than George Eliot, part of the London intelligentsia yet to some degree socially isolated because

2. Cox and Gilbert, eds., *Victorian Ghost Stories,* x; Ashley, ed., *Mrs Gaskell's Tales of Mystery and Horror,* 11; Ward, introduction to *The Works of Mrs. Gaskell,* 1:xlv–xlvi, xxxi.

she lived with a married man, G. H. Lewes, Gaskell seems more nearly the type of the Victorian angel in the house, if not indeed, to borrow Hilary M. Schor's words, "a museum piece of Victorian culture." Raised after the death of her mother in the small idyllic town of Knutsford (about which she would write in *Cranford*), married to a Unitarian minister, living thereafter in a big city where she raised four girls and entertained myriad friends, relatives, and visitors, she lived a life that appears synonymous with what Stoneman calls "the Victorian ideological 'package'" of the woman whose position included "wife- and mother-hood, submission and domesticity." Gaskell's life looks more centered and peaceful than those of her contemporaries who wrote supernatural stories, its "essential quietness, respectability and overt domesticity" leaving, according to one critic, "hardly a crevice for any sensation."[3]

Yet Gaskell's life was not as simple as it initially appears. Like her friend Charlotte Brontë and like George Eliot, whose works she admired in spite of their being written by a fornicator and adulterer, Gaskell also knew about isolation and exclusion. "A feeling of frustration and reined-in energy," as Jennifer Uglow points out in her biography of Gaskell, "was often to mark her flight into . . . [the] inner world." Although she was either befriended by or knew "Miss Marslands, Mrs Robberds, Miss Mitchell, Mrs Leisler, Mrs Mason," as well as notable figures like Charles Dickens, John Forster, William Thackeray, and Jane and Thomas Carlyle, and though she was linked through her mother to the great intellectual families of the day, the Wedgwoods, Darwins, and Turners, she was a member of a religious group scorned by other Christians for its lack of attention to dogma, for its "liberalisms." As Angus Easson puts it in his account of the opposition and hostility Unitarians experienced in a Trinitarian society, "On two great principles, Unitarianism sticks: Unity of God, to whom all worship must be paid, and Jesus's mission as a man approved by God. The appeals are to reason and the Scriptures: every man's right to his own way to God, and the wrong of state establishment. In this openness of minimal belief, beyond which lay agnosticism and atheism, are the ideas of Christianity and a Church, though many in the nineteenth century found them too vague to be the Church they wanted."

3. Charlotte Brontë names London "this big Babylon" in a letter to her friend Ellen Nussey; see Shorter, *The Brontës*, 2:96. Schor, *Scheherezade in the Marketplace: Elizabeth Gaskell and the Victorian Novel*, 4; Stoneman, *Elizabeth Gaskell*, 13; Edgar Wright, *Mrs. Gaskell: The Basis for Reassessment*, 7.

Religiously situated between the "narrowly Anglican" Charlotte Brontë and the agnostic George Eliot, Gaskell, even if she did not personally experience social ostracism, would have been intellectually aware of being an outcast in the minds of other Christians.[4]

Interestingly enough, as a Unitarian and a female, Gaskell was exempt from some of the limitations and restrictions imposed on other Christian women. Unitarians, in their "proud radicalism," which allowed "many shades of opinion," were more egalitarian than their brothers, and so the education of women was seen as as much their right and due as men's. The Unitarian faith, to use Coral Lansbury's words, "in progress and perfectibility" that could be achieved by "the power of reason to effect change" applied to women as well as to men. "To be born a woman in the Victorian era was to enter a world of social and cultural deprivation unknown to a man. But to be born a woman and Unitarian was to be released from much of the prejudice and oppression enjoined upon other women." Still, to be born a woman and a Unitarian did not release one from all such prejudice and oppression, nor did it leave one oblivious to the condition of other women, who were not happily Unitarian. Thus, as Lansbury says, "Unitarians were to be leaders in the movement for women's rights. Eliza Fox, Barbara Bodichon, Harriet Martineau, Emily Shaen and Florence Nightingale were all Unitarians of varying degrees of faith."[5]

Gaskell's religion, which one critic declares was "at the heart of her and of all she writes," buffered for her the crisis of faith and doubt that helped create for some Victorians a propitious place for the ghost story. Felicia Bonaparte, in *The Gypsy-Bachelor of Manchester*, finding that, on the contrary, Gaskell has "altogether very little" to say about religion and "is not preoccupied by it," still remarks that "unlike their neighbors," the Unitarians "walked unscathed through the Higher Criticism that was subjecting scriptural claims to historical scrutiny, remained untroubled by geological findings that challenged the biblical age of the earth, and even listened with interest to Darwin . . . whom Gaskell knew." While others "wrestled with doubts," Unitarians like Gaskell could "turn

---

4. Uglow, *Elizabeth Gaskell: A Habit of Stories*, 4; Gaskell, *The Letters of Mrs Gaskell*, letter 90, p. 144 (hereafter cited parenthetically as *LG* with letter number followed by page number); Easson, *Elizabeth Gaskell*, 6; the term "narrowly Anglican" is Wright's (*Mrs. Gaskell*, 45).

5. Uglow, *Elizabeth Gaskell*, 7; Lansbury, *Elizabeth Gaskell: The Novel of Social Crisis*, 13, 11, 13.

calmly to other things," as she does in her supernatural tales. Lansbury, also commenting on the place of religion in Gaskell's life and work, notes that "as a Unitarian Elizabeth Gaskell was unshaken by the crises of doubt and faith that troubled so many Victorians." Lansbury goes on, however, to argue, "Her lack of concern with the after-life and the nature of sin deprived her work of the metaphysical and mystical qualities common to many writers of the period. When she wrote a ghost story, the ghost was always a manifestation of someone's troubled mind. Madness was a recurring theme in her work, but Elizabeth Gaskell argued that if people believed strongly enough in the irrational then the irrational would assuredly become a reality to them." To be sure, it is as Lansbury and others observe: Gaskell was apparently unshaken by the Victorian crisis of faith. However, it does not necessarily follow that she was untouched by the crisis or that being unshaken by it she could thereby only create ghosts that were a "manifestation of someone's troubled mind." After all, Gaskell, a keen and sympathetic observer of society, was not blind to what was happening around her. As Lansbury herself elsewhere remarks, "Like her husband, Elizabeth Gaskell saw materialist and scientific doctrines triumphing in consequence of the failings of established religion."[6] Sympathetic awareness alone of her neighbors' religious dilemma could well have afforded her insight into the "metaphysical and mystical qualities" of ghosts that are more than manifestations of psychological disturbance.

In any event, though her religion was based on reason, and per-haps because of Unitarianism's "necessitarian framework" that could, as Uglow observes, "feel constricting and arid, denying feeling and mystery,"[7] scientific and materialist doctrines did not "triumph" in the life of Gaskell. Having attended the Exhibition of 1851 three times, she declared to her friend Anne Robson that she "should never care to go again; but then I'm *not* scientific nor mechanical" (*LG*, 101/159). What she much preferred was to take trips away from smoky Manchester, that industrialized center of a technologically based materialism. On one such occasion, a visit in 1849 to "Shottery, the village where Shakespeare's wife lived in her maiden days" (*LG*, 48/80), Gaskell demonstrated the

6. W. A. Craik, *Elizabeth Gaskell and the English Provincial Novel*, 4; Bonaparte, *The Gypsy-Bachelor of Manchester: The Life of Mrs. Gaskell's Demon*, 98; Lansbury, *Elizabeth Gaskell*, 8–9, 196–97.
7. Uglow, *Elizabeth Gaskell*, 6.

openness of her religion by showing herself in the broad light of day to be a seer. In a letter to her friend "Tottie" (Eliza Fox), she wrote, "I SAW a ghost! Yes I did; though in such a matter of fact place as Charlotte St I should not wonder if you are sceptical"—without pausing Gaskell continues—"and had my fortune told by a gypsy; curiously true as to the past, at any rate, and I did my duty as a meek submissive lion, fresh imported from the desert (i.e. London), at a party" (*LG*, 48/81).

The contexts of both Gaskell's report of the sighting and the sighting itself are telling. The extant portion of the letter opens with Gaskell's playful suggestion that had her friend's mesmeric clairvoyant powers been operative, those powers would have revealed Gaskell's whereabouts and condition. Gaskell refers to clairvoyance in the same bantering tone at least once more in the letter, when she also mentions with amusement not only the fortune-telling session with the gypsies but also the villagers' belief in ghosts. The result is that the reader is taken aback when she presents her own supernatural experience, not only with the vehemence and drama that the capitalized "SAW" announces but also with the brevity and sincerity of her declaration that she actually did see and not conjure up the spirit ("Yes I did"). This contrast between the bantering tone of the letter and the serious and energetic recording of her own numinous experience echoes in Gaskell's ironic recognition that something generally purported to be as unfactual and impractical as a ghost appears in such a matter-of-fact place as Charlotte Street, appears, as it were, in the Victorian noontide. Critic Margaret Ganz, who identifies Elizabeth Gaskell as an artist in conflict, would no doubt shrewdly point to Gaskell's experience as a sign of that artistic conflict. Bonaparte, disposed to see Gaskell's supernaturalism as play and Gaskell's own claims of a superstitious nature as "jest," agrees with biographer Winifred Gérin's conclusion that Gaskell's moment as a seer is "very much to be doubted" and is not "meant to be taken literally." As understandable and sensible as Bonaparte and Gérin's statements about the Shottery incident are, they are hastily dismissive. Gaskell's out-of-Manchester adventure may also be read more revealingly as evidence of her ability to entertain a more expansive or eclectic reality. After all, as Uglow has commented, "Her eye for the bizarre was as sharp as it was for the mundane."[8]

8. Bonaparte, *Gypsy-Bachelor*, 49, 110; Uglow, *Elizabeth Gaskell*, 23.

The fact that Gaskell's sighting took place in a village and not in the even more matter-of-fact Manchester is also worth noting, since most of her short stories, including her supernatural tales, are set outside the city to which she was committed but which she longed often enough to leave behind.[9] Interestingly enough, Gaskell reserved the urban setting for her fiction of social realism. Living at the heart of industrial Manchester she saw, just as surely as she saw her village ghost, the effects of change. In the "crowded bustling jostling world" (*LG*, 60/96) of changes that often resulted in getting and spending, Gaskell was well aware that the city had an energy and reality of its own, but she knew too that its socioeconomic realities could be draining.[10] Within the walls of her own home, "a mile and a half from the *very* middle of Manchester" (*LG*, 48/81), she was often "outrageously busy" (*LG*, 15/40) making arrangements for her husband's comfort and welfare, raising her daughters, supervising servants entertaining company, visiting schools, and participating on committees.[11] Outside her home, questions of labor disputes, the ills of factory work, the difficulties of manufacturers, and the impaired morality and working conditions of seamstresses raged all about Gaskell and claimed her attention. She wrote boldly and rationally about these realities in the social novels *Mary Barton* (1848), *Ruth* (1853), and *North and South* (1855), novels in which "she acts," as Craik observes, "on the faith that if facts are known, then improvement may follow, and so feels no obligation to exaggerate, or dramatize or heighten."[12]

Gaskell had a slightly different agenda in her supernatural tales, which pulsate with a drama that has been identified as "melodrama" and disparaged as Dickensian.[13] Gaskell's supernatural stories have, as

9. Craik also comments on Gaskell's "feelings of commitment to and distaste for Manchester" (*Elizabeth Gaskell and the English Provincial Novel*, 2). See also Lansbury, *Elizabeth Gaskell*, 19, 20–21.

10. See *LG*, 127/192–93, in which Gaskell complains that some individuals would rather hand over their money or their purses than give their time or effort to help others. Edgar Wright argues, "For Mrs. Gaskell, brought up in a traditional and self-contained community where the neighboring railroad 'had been vehemently petitioned against' as 'obnoxious,' then translated by marriage to the industrial centre of England . . . the fact of change was sharply and continuously brought home as a social and technological phenomenon" (*Mrs. Gaskell*, 73–74).

11. In *LG*, 137/205, Gaskell writes of "the weary, killing wearing out bustles in this life" that include "Thackeray's lectures, two dinners, one concert card party at home, killing a pig, *my* week at the school which took me into town from 9 till 12 every morning—company in the house, Isabella leaving, Wm too busy to be agreeable to my unfortunate visitors."

12. *Elizabeth Gaskell and the English Provincial Novel*, 4.

13. On Dickens's influence on Gaskell, see Lansbury, *Elizabeth Gaskell*, 96. On the one hand, "Dickens's influence upon Elizabeth Gaskell produced," according to Lansbury, "only melodrama

a matter of course, been accounted for as mere quick financial fixes or potboilers, exercises or creations tied in to her vivid imagination, to her love of the past and of legends, to "her comprehension of a different kind of haunting—the obsession with guilt and fear," or a successful "catering to the Victorian appetite for inspiring dramas, thrilling adventures, gory mysteries, and supernatural terrors."[14] While these readings of Gaskell's supernaturalism certainly shed light on her turn to this mode of writing, Schor's contention that Gaskell's "experiments with literary form led her to examine the central stories of her culture, particularly the inscription of woman as the (silent) other," comes closest to making sense of her literary experiments with the otherworldly.[15] Examining Gaskell's stories as further evidence of Victorian women's use of the supernatural to express and explore the social and cultural but especially the spiritual anxiety of the Victorian woman demonstrates how Gaskell's turn to these more occulted concerns in her supernatural stories could be as compelling as her treatments of the more public issues in her realistic fictions.

The supernatural tale was a more fitting medium for these feminine explorations because, though the ghost story in particular became standard Victorian fare, it was not a literature scrutinized and judged with the same strictness and wariness as were realistic works, which stressed, according to Patrick Brantlinger, "the primacy of material existence and . . . reject[ed] or fail[ed] to focus upon the absent, the transcendent, the unreal." Even though the nineteenth-century ghost story had its base in realism, its very nature, of course, was to treat the absent, the transcendent, and the unreal. Part of the reason the ghost story was not subjected to the same rigorous scrutiny as were historical and realistic texts is that it tended to take the form of a short story, not a particularly significant genre at the time. Bonaparte rightly identifies the short story

---

and bathos. The ghost stories she wrote in imitation of Dickens are among her worst." On the other hand, Yvonne Ffrench notes that while the bulk of Gaskell's "assiduously" written short stories were thrown "into the ready maw of [Dickens's] *Household Words* and its successors," a "miscellaneous collection of excellent thrillers and ghost stories" also resulted from Gaskell's contributions to the magazines (*Mrs. Gaskell*, 73). John McVeagh apparently agrees for the most part with Ffrench's assessment of the short stories, if not the ghost stories; he comments that "when she was writing for Dickens's *Household Words,* she produced a crop of stories which bear the marks of haste and insufficient revision" (*Elizabeth Gaskell*, 91). See also Wright, *Mrs. Gaskell*, 80.

14. See Miriam Allot's *Elizabeth Gaskell*, 12, and Wright's *Mrs. Gaskell*, 165; Margaret Ganz, *Elizabeth Gaskell: The Artist in Conflict*, 22–23.

15. *Scheherezade*, 5.

as a form in which Gaskell and other nineteenth-century novelists "felt freer to express" themselves. "Novels had for her [Gaskell] the character more of official public statements. Stories were more like private confidences." Shedding further light on the less formal and official short story, Harold Orel notes that the Victorian Age was "a richly productive literary period . . . notable for (among other things) its nurturing of the short story." However, the genre that had, Orel continues, "been ill-defined in earlier centuries . . . for much of the nineteenth century attracted little critical attention as a new and increasingly popular reading diversion. Many Victorian authors regarded it with suspicion, as a diversion from more profitable novels and plays." Still, as the century progressed, the public's attention span, according to novelist George Gissing in his *New Grub Street* (1891), would grow shorter. This development no doubt allowed for what Orel recognizes as the maturation of the short story as a "genre during the Victorian Age," a genre whose "growing popularity [among readers, if not critics] was related to the development of general-interest periodicals and a substantial need to fill columns of white space with agreeable reading-matter."[16]

The short ghost story was a form in which women more easily and readily indulged, no doubt because during the Victorian period the form was still strongly associated with the less threatening unprofessionalized storytelling, which, with its roots in the folk, had like "all folk-arts . . . grown out of the primal urge to give tongue to what has been seen, heard, experienced." The orality of folk and ghost stories made those tales a type of communal property not as valued by the literary establishment as were other written narratives.[17] Championing poetry as the highest literary form, John Stuart Mill identified the story and storytelling as rude and childish endeavors. "In what stage of the progress of society . . . is storytelling most valued," queried Mill, "and the story-teller in greatest

16. Brantlinger, *The Spirit of Reform: British Literature and Politics, 1832–1867*, 181; Bonaparte, *Gypsy-Bachelor*, 48; Orel, *The Victorian Short Story*, ix, 1–2.

17. Ruth Sawyer, *The Way of Storytellers*, 27. One reason storytelling did not acquire a professional status during the Victorian period is that it was perceived as folksy. Indeed Sawyer as late as 1942 confirmed this perception that somehow storytelling, "motivated by simple, direct folk-emotions, by imagination . . . shaped by folk-wisdom" does not belong in the realm of the intellectual, that "To bring a sophisticated attitude to a folk-art is to jeopardize it. Or rather, it is to make it into something that it is not" (27). Uglow, in *Elizabeth Gaskell*, 245, cites Dickens on the ghost story as "common property."

request and honour?—In a rude state like that of the Tartars and Arabs at this day, and of almost all nations in the earliest stages." Again Mill answered his rhetorical question: "At what age is the passion for a story, for almost any kind of story, merely as a story, the most intense? In childhood."[18] Storytelling more often than not was a way for the caretakers of children, and thus especially for women, for mothers, for nurses like Gaskell's Hester in "The Old Nurse's Story" and Brontë's Bessie in *Jane Eyre,* to amuse and to instruct their nursery charges as well as to titillate and entertain themselves.[19] What is even more relevant, the telling (not the writing) of ghost stories constituted a favorite Victorian pastime. Enlisted in the service of social parlance, the ability to relate a good ghost story was one women could cultivate as well as, if not better than, men, since it could ultimately enhance her role as domestic and social caretaker.

Gaskell was, as Dickens dubbed her, "Scheherazade," a queen of storytellers.[20] In fact, by telling and finally writing tales of the supernatural, she found a medium particularly suited to enhance her life—if not, like her Arabian counterpart, to save it—by providing her with more money. Her supernatural stories allowed her to look with heightened focus and imagination at those subjects she had to address in her more realistic works, both short and long, with more restraint and stronger consideration as to how they would be received, especially if she wanted her audience to adopt her solutions.

In "The Old Nurse's Story," "The Poor Clare," "The Doom of the Griffiths," and "Lois the Witch," Gaskell wrote supernatural tales that would do more than fill the white space of the blank page. For one thing, these works, like Eliot's *Lifted Veil,* were written during periods of stress and strain. Although "The Doom of the Griffiths," for instance, was one of Gaskell's last published supernatural tales, it was begun in the 1830s around the time that Gaskell experienced the anxieties of a new mother, plus the anxieties of a mother who had shortly before suffered the

18. "What Is Poetry?" 77.

19. Augusta Baker and Ellin Greene in *Storytelling: Art and Technique* indicate that storytelling has traditionally been an important staple of childhood. Of course, during the Victorian period, the primary caregivers of children, especially around the nursery, were the females. For more information on the use of stories in *Jane Eyre,* see Rosemarie Bodenheimer's "Jane Eyre in Search of Her Story," in Bloom, ed., *The Brontës,* 155–68.

20. See Schor, *Scheherezade,* 3, 9.

disappointment of a stillbirth. The timing of Gaskell's other supernatural stories tends to coincide with the publication of longer works. Thus, her premier supernatural tale, "The Old Nurse's Story," a special Christmas number for Dickens's *Household Words,* was published in 1852 after her first novel *Mary Barton* (1848) and just before *Cranford* (1851–1853) and *Ruth* (1853), this last a novel about the risqué figure of the fallen woman. The remainder of Gaskell's supernatural stories appeared while she was preoccupied with her 1857 biography of Charlotte Brontë, an undertaking that caused her no small amount of anxiety, an undertaking, it should be noted, in which she depicted Charlotte as so "finely-strung" that she shrank from Gaskell's relation of "some dismal ghost story," confessing that one such vivid tale had "mingled with her dreams at night, and made her sleep restless and unrefreshing." "The Poor Clare" was published in 1856, a year after the publication of *North and South* and the death of Charlotte Brontë. The last supernatural story, "Lois the Witch," which appeared in 1859, closely followed *The Life of Charlotte Brontë.* The biography of her friend Charlotte had occasioned a furor the likes of which Gaskell would never experience again. Uglow reveals the extent of the pressure and difficulty that resulted from the Brontë project when she remarks that Gaskell "was on safer ground . . . when she passed on stories which were *not* about people she knew, like wild adventures or ghost stories . . . [which she told] constantly, with great relish."[21]

The supernatural story not only provided an artistic decompression of sorts but also, by its very nature, allowed Gaskell and others who wrote in this vein more license. After all, in addressing an issue such as ghosts—on which the patriarchal jury was either out or had declared, as did Huxley and Cruikshank, the subject to consist of childish, subjective womanish fancies—men, but particularly women, were at liberty to imagine spirit, self, and others in ways that may have seemed at a great remove from empirical fact yet managed to provide a powerful if spectral exegesis of social, cultural, and spiritual realities. This is finally to say that while Gaskell did not necessarily discontinue her rational explorations of what have been called "the unadorned realities of the industrial age,"[22] she could conduct these with more liveliness.

21. Gaskell, *The Life of Charlotte Brontë,* 380; Uglow, *Elizabeth Gaskell,* 244.
22. McVeagh, *Elizabeth Gaskell,* 3.

Gaskell did not merely cater to but rather capitalized upon the Victorian fascination with the supernatural to isolate and explore more intensely and dramatically—because at a remove from both her long social novels and her short realistic tales—the phenomena of power and the interrelations of women. Thus, even in one of her earliest supernatural tales, "Doom of the Griffiths," written in the 1830s though published in 1858, Gaskell was already beginning to develop the ideas she would repeatedly use to examine women and power—prophecy, curse, the figure of the witch. For though "Doom of the Griffiths" ostensibly presents the story of how the fate of the ninth generation of Griffiths is worked out through a father and son, a closer look at the story shows that the fate of these men depends to no insignificant degree on the women in their lives. Thus, when Augharad, Squire Robert Griffiths's daughter by his first marriage and Owen Griffiths's sister, marries and leaves the Griffiths household, it becomes clear that her domestic powers had increasingly come to underpin not just the organization of the home but also the relations between father and son.

> She had performed so many thoughtful, noiseless little offices, on which their daily comfort depended; and, now she was gone, the household seemed to miss the spirit that peacefully kept it in order; the servants roamed about in search of commands and directions; the rooms had no longer the unobtrusive ordering of taste to make them cheerful; the very fires burned dim, and were always sinking down into dull heaps of grey ashes.[23]

Despite the very real and quotidian arrangements she has made for the Griffiths men, Augharad is no more than a "spirit" in the Griffiths household and in the text itself. Yet as invisible or "unobtrusive" as she has been, she has exerted power—ordering, commanding, and directing—all noiselessly. When young Owen later marries the initially worldly and coquettish Nest Pritchard, she is transformed into Undine, becoming more like Augharad, with the ability to quietly and soberly manage Owen's physical comfort and with the power to undo "angry words and unkind actions" ("Doom," 257). Like George Eliot's Latimer, who in his marriage to Bertha seeks to recover the love and warmth of

---

23. Gaskell, "The Doom of the Griffiths," in *The Works of Mrs. Gaskell*, 5:244; hereafter cited parenthetically as "Doom."

the mother, so Owen seeks to do so through Nest, who, he assures the squire, is as pure as "the dear, precious mother who brought me forth" ("Doom," 260).

Despite the angelic ministrations of Nest, whom Owen, fearing his father's disapproval, keeps sequestered and hidden, the doom of the Griffiths (son will kill father) works itself out in great part because of the insidious powers of the squire's second wife, the stepmother whom Owen perceives to be a succubus casting a wicked spell over his father:

> a great change had taken place in the outward manifestations of his father's character; and, by degrees, Owen traced this change to the influence of his stepmother . . . [who] sacrificed the show of authority for the power. . . . His father was fast losing his temperate habits, and frequent intoxication soon took its usual effect upon the temper. Yet even here was the spell of his wife upon him. Before her he placed a restraint upon his passion, yet she was perfectly aware of his irritable disposition, and directed it hither and thither with the same apparent ignorance of the tendency of her words. ("Doom," 246)

The words of the squire's strikingly beautiful wife ("Doom," 245) propel him toward the realization of the curse, if they are not indeed a curse in and of themselves. Certainly beauty here transforms the squire into a beast, as the squire unwittingly acts on behalf of his demon lover.

Although the women in this story are essentially as noiseless and unobtrusive, as occulted, as those in Mary Shelley's *Frankenstein*—another text in which the women though present are portrayed as passive unto death—their influence and powers are "paramount, if unacknowledged" ("Doom," 265).[24] In succeeding stories Gaskell continued not only to treat the subject of women and power but also to give women greater presence, voice, and contact with each other.

In her earliest published and most anthologized supernatural tale, "The Old Nurse's Story," Gaskell, as Uglow points out, "produced a bold, sweeping treatment of the same themes—unmarried sex and illegitimacy—that she was currently dealing with so cautiously in *Ruth*."[25] However, "The Old Nurse's Story" is finally more than the overflow from

24. U. C. Knoepflmacher recognizes in *Frankenstein* the "equation of femininity with a passivity that borders on the ultimate passivity of death" ("Thoughts on the Aggression of Daughters," 108).
25. *Elizabeth Gaskell,* 307.

Ruth, as Gaskell this time presents a family history in which women's relations to each other prove strikingly more prominent than those represented in "Doom of the Griffiths." Hester, the nurse and narrator in the 1852 tale, straightaway recalls her powerful attachment to her orphaned charge, Miss Rosamond, and her determination to go "with the little child to the end of the world."[26] She finds, just as forty-six years later Henry James's governess in *Turn of the Screw* would discover, that such a commitment can land her not only at the end of the world but indeed in the otherworld. Hester's love of Rosamond certainly occasions her great anxiety and suffering, which, interestingly enough, have their source in and mirror the connection the child Rosamond forms with the phantom child in the lane. Just as Hester, who is no more than a child herself ("I was not eighteen"), still delighting in hide-and-seek, is prepared to follow Rosamond into the distant, desolate, and neglected "wilderness of a [haunted] house" where old Miss Furnivall and her companion and maid, Mrs. Stark, sit working like two furies "at the same great piece of tapestry," so Rosamond is prepared to follow the specter child up to the snow-covered death trap, the Fells, where the spectral child's mother, the dead sister of Miss Furnivall, sits weeping and waiting ("Old Nurse's," 424, 429, 427, 426).

Although Hester agonizes over her charge's excursion with the ghost (Rosamond nearly dies as a result of her attentions to the little phantom girl), the suffering she and Rosamond undergo is preferable to the pains the strong and proud Miss Furnivall experiences as she seeks to disconnect herself from Maude, her equally proud and contentious, though now dead, sister. She had competed with Maude for the affections of the foreign music master. In a jealous rage she had revealed to her father the secret of her older sister's marriage to and child by the music teacher, who had by this time deserted his wife and child. By getting her sister Maude banished from the house and put out onto the Fells, where the child soon dies, Miss Furnivall, like the squire's wife in "Doom of the Griffiths," who eventually if indirectly turns Owen out of his own home, commits a demonic and heinous act for which she is feared as one belonging to or at least consorting with the otherworld: "All this time I

26. "The Old Nurse's Story," in *The Works of Mrs. Gaskell,* 2:423; hereafter cited parenthetically as "Old Nurse's."

kept away from Miss Furnivall and Mrs. Stark, as much as ever I could; for I feared them—I knew no good could be about them, with their grey, hard faces, and their dreamy eyes, looking back into the ghastly years that were gone" ("Old Nurse's," 442).

Miss Furnivall has sinned, but not against the father; she has sinned against the mother, against woman and sister. For while the females in this story tend to need protection and assistance (Rosamond is orphaned; Maude and her child are deserted by the musician and then disowned by Mr. Furnivall), not the males in the story, who after all are absent, but the females have it more immediately within their power to be compassionate and to provide succor.[27] So the nurse fiercely and passionately cares for "my little lady—my lamb—my queen—my darling" ("Old Nurse's," 434), and the phantom child leads Rosamond to the ghost of Maude so that that spectral woman will stop her weeping and hungering for a live child about which she can wrap her arms, and even Dorothy, who presides over the kitchen, welcomes Hester and Rosamond with great warmth and affection. But Miss Furnivall, who has spent most of her eighty years shutting out and destroying her sister, finally closing off the very wing in which Maude had lived, never connects with any real warmth to another woman.

Looking back, Hester, now nurse to Rosamond's children, recalls that even Miss Furnivall's relations to the one woman who has remained by her through the years, her personal servant Mrs. Stark, had not developed into a full-blown, nurturing friendship, although

> sitting with her [Grace Furnivall] . . . was Mrs. Stark, her maid and companion, and almost as old as she was. She had lived with Miss Furnivall ever since they were both young, and now she seemed more like a friend than a servant; she looked so cold, and grey, and stony, as if she had never loved or cared for any one; and I don't suppose she did care for any one, except her mistress; and, owing to the great deafness of the latter, Mrs. Stark treated her very much as if she were a child. ("Old Nurse's," 426)

27. Males have deeply affected Miss Furnivall's life. Maude and Grace's father, old man Furnivall, for example, ruled with strength, pride, and hardness before his demise. Miss Furnivall's confinement ultimately grows out of the rejection she experiences at the hands of a male, the musician who marries her sister instead of her. It is worth noting that such rejection and the subsequent jealousy do not arise in *Cranford*, in which the younger sister, Matilda, relinquishes her lover because her older sister disapproves of the choice.

Her eyes blinded by passion, her ears stopped up with pride, jealousy, and hatred, Grace Furnivall was unable to sympathize with the sister who, though equally fierce in her pride and hatred, suffered cruelly when she had found herself helpless to prevent the child she "loved . . . to distraction" from being deserted, abused, stricken, driven along with herself out of the house into a snowstorm ("Old Nurse's," 440). Now Miss Furnivall's youthful and willful blindness and deafness have been replaced by a natural deafness that keeps her from hearing Mrs. Stark, who thereby treats her more like a child than a good and cherished friend.

Herein lies the crux of the old nurse's story. It is fitting that Grace Furnivall ends up being identified, if only briefly, as childlike, because more horrible than the spectral reenactment of the banishment, than the ghost mother weeping on the Fells, than the organ music that causes Hester to shiver in the noontide, is Miss Furnivall's refusal to help even her young niece, who is turned out of the house. In the story Miss Furnivall is held more culpable than old Mr. Furnivall for sending away and making a ghost both figuratively and literally of Maude's child. Significantly, the child, not the mother, returns to the Furnivall mansion and, like the ghost of Emily Brontë's Catherine, entreats that she be let in. In this tale, as in "Doom of the Griffiths," in which Robert Griffiths kills his own grandchild, the child has been the hapless victim who could have been spared, if ultimately women like the squire's wife and here Grace Furnivall had acted as good nurses or nurturers. Instead, the child is doomed to ghosthood because there is no hearing, saving, or healing where there is not enough love, but especially where women are at odds. There can be no salvation, or affection, or freedom where there is no sisterhood.[28]

In her next two stories, "The Poor Clare" and "Lois the Witch," Gaskell used the figure of the witch to advance her study of women's relations to each other and to power. Generally understood to be a woman who sold her soul for power, the witch could be found, like the angel, at the hearth; however, she was said to brew potions there, not boil tripe. She proffered a compelling contrast to the angel in the house, for unlike the Victorian angel, the witch consorted with demons, even engaged in sex

28. See Uglow's deft handling of Gaskell and friendships between women in *Elizabeth Gaskell*, 164–65.

with them. Unlike the angel who lovingly tended the children, the witch was rumored to have sacrificed them. Witches used their brooms to fly off to midnight meetings, not to sweep the patriarchal floor. While these specific aspects of the witch are not necessarily those Gaskell highlighted in her stories, the perverseness associated with this figure and the power the witch could wield, particularly through her words, was a subject that would intrigue her in such stories as "The Poor Clare" and "Lois the Witch."

Although the witch craze in England had run its course by the end of the seventeenth century and the idea of the angel in the house held sway in the nineteenth, witches and what one critic has termed a pseudo-religious witchcraft still held a spot in the consciousness of an age fascinated with mesmerism and spiritualism.[29] Ultimately, what Montague Summers in his *Geography of Witchcraft* wrote some twenty years after the close of the nineteenth century was generally no less true of or pertinent to the Victorian age than his own: "In our towns never was Witchcraft more openly and more unblushingly practised than at the present time, for what is Modern Spiritism with its mediums and materializations but Old Witchcraft writ Large? There is hardly a phenomenon of these sabbat-séances to-day that cannot be exactly paralleled in the witch-trials of the seventeenth century."[30] Yet the idea of witches was one that did not surface as often in the nineteenth century as one might suspect, certainly not as often as did the subject of ghosts, perhaps because witches were so strikingly antithetical to the more current notion of the angel at the hearth.

In her study of the myths of Victorian womanhood, Nina Auerbach identifies "four central types" in Victorian iconography—"the angel, the demon, the old maid, and the fallen woman."[31] Auerbach also mentions more specifically mermaids, serpents, fairies, goblins, and vampires. Although the witch is certainly implicit in some of these icons and falls under the type of the demon, the fact that Auerbach makes scant mention of witchcraft in her text and does not focus on the type or icon

29. J. W. Wickwar, *Witchcraft and the Black Art*, 14.

30. *The Geography of Witchcraft*, 180. See also the Goldfarbs, who note a biblical connection between witches, wizards, spiritualism, and mesmerism in their observations about the Witch of Endor (*Spiritualism and Nineteenth-Century Letters*, 19).

31. *Woman and the Demon*, 63.

of the witch not only expresses her own findings about the old maid (who when "written about sympathetically [during the Victorian era] . . . generally moves from a Gothic to a gently pathetic figure, shedding her tokens of witchcraft to become a plaintiff variant of the angel in the house") but also suggests that the association of witches and women, indeed the very notion of witchcraft, was an idea Victorians wanted to put behind them or felt themselves above. Witchcraft, however, was not so easily packed away because it was part of what Diana Basham identifies as "a long tradition of associations which, throughout the nineteenth century, linked the growth of feminist consciousness with the history of the Victorian occult revival." Unsurprisingly then, witchcraft resurfaced during the nineteenth century; furthermore, when it did resurface it was often enough reconstituted, Basham notes, as mesmerism, the very mesmerism, I might add, that Jane Carlyle had declared to be "all of one family with witchcraft, demoniacal possession."[32]

Still, there were some interesting nineteenth-century works on witchcraft that ultimately help us appreciate and assess the singularity of Gaskell's witch stories. At the beginning of the Victorian period, Sir Walter Scott contributed to John Murray's Family Library series his *Letters on Demonology and Witchcraft* (1830), about which Harriet Martineau six years later would give, if not a scathing review, then a tepid one. What Martineau does and does not say in her review finally lends support to the idea that Victorians were not wont to dwell on the notion of witches. Martineau bemoaned the fact that Scott had missed the opportunity to dispel superstition. "What an opportunity has he lost of illustrating a dark region of life!" she wrote. "Sir Walter Scott, by uniting the philosophy and the poetry as we expected he would, might have produced a work of singular interest and beauty, instead of doing what in him lay to set back the world which he has such mighty power to roll onward."[33] However, instead of exploring for herself more closely the superstitions surrounding witches, their relations to demons, or women's connection to the idea of demons or witches, Martineau used the review to argue against the idea of ghosts.

32. Ibid., 111; Auerbach also comments that the "socially conscious Victorians averted their minds from the demonic contagion with which an earlier age had invested spinsterhood" (110). Basham, *Trial of Woman,* 2, 75–77.
33. "Demonology and Witchcraft," in *Miscellanies,* 2:113.

Some twenty years later, in 1861, Eliza Lynn Linton would at least remain focused on the idea of witches as she garnered, in what may be one of the best collections of witch stories presented to the Victorian public, a collection more distinguished, or at least more familiar, than Lady Jane Wilde's or Mary L. Lewes's works on this subject.[34] In her preface Linton suggests that she is one of the first to undertake the difficult task of addressing the idea of witches by editing a volume exclusively dedicated to historical accounts of "the demonic contagion":

> In offering the following collection of witch stories to the public, I do not profess to have exhausted the subject, or to have made so complete a summary as I might have done, had I been admitted into certain private libraries, which contain, I believe, many concealed riches. But I had no means of introduction to them, and was obliged to be content with such authorities as I found in the British Museum, and the other public libraries to which I had access. I do not think that I have left much untold; but there must be, scattered about England, old MSS. and unique copies of records concerning which I can find only meagre allusions, or the mere names of the victims, without a distinctive fact to mark their special history.

Linton claims to have undertaken the difficult task of gathering the stories so that every reader might "judge for himself" the truth and nature of witchcraft. Yet, like Martineau's review of Scott's *Demonology and Witchcraft,* her collection, *Witch Stories,* is finally a protest against the credulity and supernaturalism of the day:

> But the snake is scotched, not killed. So far are we in advance of the men of the ruder past, inasmuch as our superstitions, though quite as silly, are less cruel than theirs, and hurt no one but ourselves.... And as it seems to me that credulity is even a less desirable frame of mind than scepticism, I have set forth this collection of witch stories as landmarks of the excesses to which a blind belief may hurry and impel humanity, and perhaps as some slight aids to that much misused common sense which the holders of impossible theories generally

34. For more information on Victorian women who wrote factually or fictively about witches and witchcraft, see Peter Haining, ed., *A Circle of Witches: An Anthology of Victorian Witchcraft Stories.* In identifying Victorian women writers "devoted to British witchcraft history" (12), Haining refers specifically to Linton's *Witch Stories,* Wilde's *Ancient Legends, Mystic Charms and Superstitions of Ireland,* and Mary Lewis's [Lewes's] *The Queer Side of Things.*

consider "enthusiastic," and of "a nobler life" to tread under foot, and loftily ignore.[35]

For Linton the idea of witchcraft was finally a crude and silly superstition that common sense, if allowed, would rout.

In comparison to Linton's historical collection of witch stories, Gaskell's fictional treatment of witchcraft, and more particularly of the witch, looks much more ambiguous as she marks that which neither Martineau nor Linton singled out: the troubled area of women's communion. Like the narrator Hester in "The Old Nurse's Story," Bridget Fitzgerald in "The Poor Clare" is nurse to another female. By the time we see Bridget she is "a woman past middle age . . . with a firm and strong step,"[36] following her now grown and married charge from Antwerp to Lancashire. Unlike the character of Hester in "The Old Nurse's Story" (not the older Hester who serves as narrator), Bridget is not a young woman who delights in children's games like hide-and-seek. She is mature and serious, a more memorable and striking character than that more ideal type of the English nursemaid, Hester. For one thing, Bridget is not only a pious Roman Catholic but also an outlandish foreigner and a passionate mother, vehement of gesture, fierce of will, full of pride. "Excepting for the short period of her own married life, Bridget Fitzgerald had never left her nursling" ("Poor Clare," 333); her loyalty has netted both her and her daughter great influence, as they have "moved from one house to the other at [their] own will" and "had great influence over [Mrs. Starkley] and, through her, over her husband" ("Poor Clare," 334). Having so bonded with her charge, Bridget is able to "exert . . . despotic power" that the other servants perceive and fear as they "yielded to her 'magic of a superior mind' " ("Poor Clare," 334). Only Bridget's daughter, Mary, rebels against Bridget, and the story and its supernatural events have their basis in the troubled, if not ruptured, bond between the mother and daughter.

In the story, so unlike "Old Nurse's," in which Rosamond is Hester's all in all, it is Mary and not Lady Starkley who is Bridget's "little lady . . . lamb . . . queen . . . darling." "Bridget's love for her child lay very deep— deeper than that daughter ever knew; or, I should think, she would never

35. Linton, ed., *Witch Stories*, iii, iv, 426–28.

36. "The Poor Clare," in *The Works of Mrs. Gaskell*, 5:332; hereafter cited parenthetically as "Poor Clare."

have wearied of home as she did, and prayed her mistress [Starkley] to obtain for her some situation" ("Poor Clare," 334). In contrast to Old Miss Furnivall, who is apparently incapable of loving another female, be it her sister or her niece, Bridget loves so fiercely that in the course of uncanny events that love becomes supernaturally hurtful. Mary leaves home, has a child, and dies; the father of that child, Squire Gisborne, visits Lancashire, where he wantonly shoots and kills the dog that had been Mary's favorite. Bridget, unaware that she has a grandchild and that Gisborne is the father of that child, "fix[es] his unwilling, sullen look, with her dark and terrible eye" ("Poor Clare," 340) and curses him, thereby blindly cursing her own grandchild.

Bridget Fitzgerald's strength, foreign habit, and unsociable demeanor, the unannounced trips she makes, suddenly leaving her home for months to search for her daughter, then just as suddenly reappearing— these do not conform to the image of the passive, gentle, dependent, homebound angel in the house. Instead, Bridget's unorthodox behavior and especially her appearance are suggestive of the witchlike crone:

> she looked as if she had been scorched in the flames of hell, so brown, and scared, and fierce a creature did she seem. By and-by [*sic*] many saw her; and those who met her eye once cared not to be caught looking at her again. She had got into the habit of perpetually talking to herself; nay, more, answering herself, and varying her tones according to the side she took at the moment. It was no wonder that those who dared to listen outside her door at night believed that she held converse with some spirit; in short, she was unconsciously earning for herself the dreadful reputation of a witch. ("Poor Clare," 338–39)

This realistic and reasonable account of how Bridget may have seemed a witch is almost immediately undercut when indeed Bridget curses and the curse is borne out.

In "The Poor Clare" and in "Lois the Witch" it is the daughters who pay for the sins of the father. More important, in "The Poor Clare" it is the female, Lucy Gisborne, who pays for the sins of the mother. In this case the sin of the mother lies in willfulness, pride, and "latent" power, in her ability "to catalyze the liminality of [her] inscription within the larger social order to draw upon forces and mechanisms outside the orthodox belief systems."[37] To put it another way, the mother's sin lies

37. See Regina Barreca's discussion of sorcery and curses in "Writing as Voodoo," 187, 177.

in daring to lift her voice against the male. Just as Bridget and her daughter have been split asunder by the despotism of the former and the rebellion of the latter, so when Bridget curses Gisborne and thereby her own granddaughter, Lucy, that granddaughter is split asunder too, as she becomes haunted by her opposite. The "pure," "holy," "simple," "saintly" Lucy is persecuted by another, "loathsome," "mocking and voluptuous" destructive self, one capable of desecrating nature and sullying her own self by "dancing over the tender plants in the flower-beds" and becoming unduly familiar with the grooms ("Poor Clare," 363, 357, 359, 362, 360, 361). The division of her grandchild into a madonna and a whore, while it mirrors the rupture between the mother who wanted her Mary to stay at home and the child who wanted to go out (and does go out to experience the world, even sexually), also reflects the two faces of Bridget, who was "no common woman" but "one powerful for good as for evil" ("Poor Clare," 378).

In order to save Lucy from the doppelgänger, in order to put an end to the division begun by her split with Mary, Bridget, who has indeed by this time come to resemble the classic portrait of a witch—"Her teeth were all gone, so the nose and chin were brought near together; the grey eyebrows were straight, and almost hung over her deep, cavernous eyes, and the thick white hair lay in silvery masses over the low, wide, wrinkled forehead" ("Poor Clare," 346)—this cronelike Bridget must don the robes of the sisterhood of Poor Clares and become Sister Magdalen. Bridget must give up her proud and powerful self, but more important, she must give up her voice to become a communal angel in the house: "Henceforward her former self must be buried . . . but never more to make sign, or utter cry on earth! She has become a Poor Clare, in order that, by perpetual penance and constant service of others, she may at length so act as to obtain final absolution and rest for her soul" ("Poor Clare," 381). Making the ultimate sacrifice of her powerful, energetic, demonic self and voice, even as she nurses back to health the sinning pale-unto-death Gisborne, the willful Bridget dies, so that Lucy may be an unequivocally untainted angel.

Miss Furnivall, Dorothy the servant, and Hester the nurse ultimately rally around Miss Rosamond in "The Old Nurse's Story." In "The Poor Clare," while Lucy's doppelgänger drives away her own father and even while Lucy's lover, the narrator, confesses, "I shrink from her ever since that day on the moor-side. And men must shrink from one so accompanied; friends and lovers must stand afar off" ("Poor Clare," 374)—while the men can barely stand the knowledge of a Lucy who is no angel, the women in the story are the agents who see her through the demonic ordeal. Only "my dear and faithful Mistress Clarke" ("Poor Clare," 359) is able to remain constantly by Lucy's side, and of course Bridget Fitzgerald works out both Lucy's and her own salvation.

In "Lois the Witch," Gaskell's last published supernatural story, a historical piece based upon Charles Upham's, William Howitt's, and Harriet Martineau's works on witchcraft and set in the time of the Salem trials, no woman comes to Lois's assistance in the end.[38] On the contrary, Lois is divested of woman-love, and herein lies her doom. For "Lois the Witch" explores among other things "female solidarity" or the lack thereof.[39] Gaskell most strongly signals the breakdown in female relations in the one supernatural incident that informs what could have otherwise been read as a realistic portrayal of destructive superstition. When the English parson's young daughter, Lois—held high in the arms of her nurse, who has joined a crowd to watch the dunking of one old woman rumored to be a witch—catches the eye of the unfortunate old woman, Hannah, Hannah curses Lois: "Parson's wench, parson's wench, yonder, in thy nurse's arms, thy dad hath never tried for to save me; and none shall save thee, when thou art brought up for a witch."[40] Although the old woman perceives her persecutor to be a patriarch, the male representative of the church, she transfers her resentment to the girl-child. Old Hannah is the first of a number of women in this story whose troubled or disrupted relations to a male are diverted into negative emotions and actions against another female, namely Lois. Gaskell uses the supernatural to underscore an exchange between women that will be repeated with as much devastation as the ghostly reenactment of the sister-hatred Hester witnesses in "The Old Nurse's Story."

38. In *Elizabeth Gaskell*, 475, Uglow notes that "the story follows the rationalist analysis of witchcraft trials as examples of medical and priestly obscurantism that had engaged Unitarians in the 1830s—an approach evident, for instance, in Gaskell's chief source, *Lectures on Witchcraft* (1831) by Charles Upham, the Unitarian minister in Salem, in William Howitt's popular history of priestcraft (1833) and in Harriet Martineau's lucid article on Salem (1834)." Gaskell also left fragments of two other supernatural tales.

39. Tess Cosslett uses this expression in *Woman to Woman: Female Friendship in Victorian Fiction*.

40. "Lois the Witch," in *The Works of Mrs. Gaskell*, 7:122; hereafter cited parenthetically as "Lois."

Even Lois's mother demonstrates how women's relations to men can, if only momentarily, undercut female solidarity. After Lois's father, Parson Barclay, dies, Lois's mother, on her own deathbed, for one brief but very human and selfish moment, puts her dead husband before her living child, as she advises Lois to seek a home with her brother. "'Write to him as soon as I am gone—for, Lois, I am going; and I bless the Lord that has letten me join my husband again so soon.' Such was the selfishness of conjugal love; she little thought of Lois's desolation in comparison with her rejoicing over her speedy reunion with her dead husband!" ("Lois," 112). Although Gaskell makes it clear that Mrs. Barclay loves Lois, this shift from motherly compassion to conjugal selfishness adumbrates one duality in the story that ultimately further advances an examination of how females' relations to males may be implicated in, or better yet, may haunt their relations to other females.

Two households in the New World, the one where Lois spends a night on her way to reside with her American relatives and that of her relatives, the Hicksons, reflect the dualism of love and selfishness anticipated in the mother's parting words to Lois. Both households are essentially not only headed by females but also ultimately centered in females. Widow Smith, with two daughters, has "a kind of authority which no one liked to disobey" once she made decisions about the guests she would admit to her home. Smith especially "was a privileged person" who enjoyed "the liberty of speech which was tacitly denied to many, under penalty of being esteemed ungodly" ("Lois," 115, 117). Grace Hickson, with her two daughters, her son, and a bedridden husband who has "never had the force of character that Grace, his spouse, possessed," becomes a widow almost as soon as Lois moves in and may just as well have been one even when her husband lived for all the authority he wielded around the house ("Lois," 128). Grace Hickson's son, Manasseh, her favorite child, if not her obsession, is described as the "real head of the house"; however, though Manasseh is definitely a presence in the household where "his word was law with his grim mother," he is a ghost- or seerlike figure who "was little in the house," who "sat quiet and silent where he did, with the book open upon his knee; his eyes thoughtfully fixed on vacancy, as if he saw a vision, or dreamed dreams" ("Lois," 133, 127, 133, 130). With two males whose abilities to fill the traditional male role as head of the household are so circumscribed by physical and mental debilities,

Grace, with "a deep voice, almost as masculine as her son's," appears to be the real force and wield the real power in the Hickson household ("Lois," 126). The tall, stern, angular, masculine-voiced Grace Hickson is the opposite of the "comely, motherly" Widow Smith with her "knack of making every one beneath her roof comfortable and at his ease" ("Lois," 115). After the warm, motherly reception Lois receives from Widow Smith, the "ungracious reception" she gets from her Aunt Grace only heightens the sense of loss and desolation Lois experiences as one recently orphaned, separated from the man she loves, and newly arrived in America ("Lois," 126).

Instead of finding love and support in the Hickson household, instead of finding sisterhood among the females—Grace and her daughters—Lois comes to find herself among enemies more formidable and insidious than the Indians and pirates she had heard about at Widow Smith's dinner table. Ironically the Hicksons identify Lois's home in England with her Jacobinic father and mother as a house of the ungodly. Consequently, they treat her like an outcast and an outsider as reprehensible as any Indian or pirate. Initially, one of the main reasons the Hicksons do not accept Lois is because they view her religious beliefs as ungodly. But it becomes clear that Lois's difficulties among the Hicksons arise also from the way other women in the family view her relations to significant males. In short, they feel that Lois somehow is pirating the affections or attentions of the men whose attentions and affections they covet for themselves. So Faith Hickson, the cousin Lois wants to look upon as a sister ("Lois," 180), despises Lois because young Pastor Nolan is attracted to the English girl. Similarly, Grace Hickson, "a woman of narrow, strong affections," resents "the stranger under her roof," not only because Lois is a "prelatist and a stranger" but also and most significantly because she fiercely disapproves of Manasseh's attraction to Lois, so much so that when Grace finds her only and mentally disturbed son proposing marriage to an unwilling Lois, she "came hastily forwards and, lifting up her strong right arm, smote their joined hands in twain, in spite of the fervour of Manasseh's grasp" ("Lois," 131, 201, 156, 155). Unsurprisingly, when Grace's impish younger daughter, Prudence, in a ploy to gain the attentions of the church fathers, accuses Lois of witchcraft, Grace Hickson, to protect her mad son and vent her anger, eagerly jumps at the chance to convince others and herself that Lois has bewitched both her younger daughter, Prudence, and her only son, her two favorites.

Gaskell disposes of all the male characters in the story who could have assisted Lois, so that the drama is played out among women. When Lois is accused of witchery, Captain Holderness, the fatherly seaman who transported Lois to America, is at sea; Ralph Lucy, Lois's betrothed, is in England. The only male who could save Lois is Manasseh, who has prophesied that Lois will die unless she marries him. Interestingly enough, however true his supernatural insights, Manasseh can no more help Lois than Eliot's seer Latimer can change Bertha. In the story women's words prove more powerful than the masculine desire for Lois's salvation. The male prophet is no match for the witch, or at least Manasseh's open-ended prophecy is subsumed by the original prophetic curse of the old woman persecuted as a witch. Indeed, Lois has experienced a succession of curses out of the mouths of women: old Hannah's declaration that Lois will die as a witch, Grace Hickson's condemnation of Lois as ungodly and strange, Faith's malicious suggestion to Prudence that Lois "has bought success in this world, and we are but her slaves," and her warning to her little sister that she "Take care, another time, how you meddle with a witch's things" ("Lois," 180–81). The culmination of this crescendo of condemnation is the accusatory speech of Prudence Hickson. It is the Hickson women who have the power to save Lois. Instead, in a story all too bereft of characters like Widow Smith, the three jealous, self-seeking kinswomen create the image of Lois as a witch, an image she herself sometimes entertains, an image that costs her her life, thereby fulfilling the prophecy of her untimely death.

The last supernatural story Gaskell had a chance to complete and publish, "Lois the Witch" powerfully demonstrates the extent to which Gaskell used the supernatural story to explore women's relations and women's power. One meaningful source of power for women, she suggested, especially in her last two published tales, was in the word.[41] Because in Victorian society good words about a woman's character were as necessary to her as breath, it is no wonder that the word in Gaskell's stories could take on the supernatural dimension of the curse. As Regina

41. What I am calling the "word" approximates what Uglow recognizes as "a *language* of their own" in a chapter entitled "Men, Women, Language, and Power" (*Elizabeth Gaskell*, 467).

Barreca has observed, "Women have a particular and complex relation to language because they have for so long been barred from acting on their ambitions or rebellions that they have learned to turn to language as a way of dealing with and influencing the world."[42] All too often characters in Gaskell's supernatural stories, especially female ones, use their words to destructive ends, often abusing each other when in fact the appropriate objects of their verbal attacks should be the likes of the musician in "The Old Nurse's Story," or the New England patriarchs such as Pastor Tappau and "Dr. Cotton Mather himself" who try Lois Barclay as a witch (182). But even when women like Bridget Fitzgerald do aim their anathemas at the heads of the squires, the negativism of women's words can rebound with ruinous effects for themselves and those they love.

The power Gaskell grants these discontented women is at best, then, a double-edged sword. Those women who wield it as well as those women who are affected by it pay dearly as power turns to powerlessness in these stories. Grace Furnivall of "The Old Nurse's Story" dies lamenting her helplessness: "Alas! alas! what is done in youth can never be undone in age! What is done in youth can never be undone in age!" ("Old Nurse's," 445). In "The Poor Clare," Bridget Fitzgerald, too, comes to feel a sense of powerlessness. She starts out as a strong-willed passionate woman and a privileged, respectable, domineering servant; she ends up a poor, humble, dependent Poor Clare. She first loses control over her daughter, who leaves. Next, after cursing the soldier Gisborne and discovering that she has thus inadvertently cursed her granddaughter, Bridget realizes that she is powerless to control even her words and that, like old Miss Furnivall, she cannot undo what has been done, at least not alone and not without great sacrifice. Like Bridget, the squire's wife in "Doom of the Griffiths" and Grace Hickson in "Lois the Witch" are strong women given power that gets out of hand. These power-wielding female characters pay for their power. Bridget dies in the expiation of her sin. Old Hannah dies even as she curses Lois. Grace Hickson loses the thing she prizes most in life, her son Manasseh.

Mystery had always attracted Gaskell. As her biographers and critics have noted, she was a lover of old legends and customs. One of her

---

42. "Writing as Voodoo," 176.

earliest written pieces is the ghoulish story of a young girl walled up and later discovered with a chunk bitten out of her shoulder, revealing how the young creature had tried to appease her hunger and perhaps symbolizing how women so confined become of necessity destructive, preying on themselves. This tale in conjunction with the curses and witchcraft of some of the later supernatural stories invites Edgar Wright's assertion that "There is an obvious link between her love of tradition and legend and her delight in ghost stories and morbidly tinged tales."[43] But Wright does not say anything of which Gaskell herself is not aware. Indeed, in a letter to Eliza Fox, Gaskell recognized art as a career that "keeps them [women] from being morbid." She was aware of a morbidity within Victorian women chained to "home duties," because she herself felt the "small Lilliputian arrows" of daily cares pricking her (LG, 68/106).

In the supernatural, especially in her witch tales, Gaskell found relief from the roles of wife, mother, and housekeeper and from what Bonaparte, reading "the whole of Elizabeth Gaskell—her life, her letters, and her fiction—as one continuous metaphoric text," calls Gaskell's "ideal," an ideal in conflict with her demon, one of the images of which is the witch.[44] In the supernatural, Gaskell found not only temporary relief from the ideal but also a measure of release from the quotidian, the rational, the material. For though her duties as model wife of Manchester's Reverend Gaskell required both her unprotesting presence in the "misty foggy Manchester, which gives me a perpetual headache very hard to bear," and a polite decorous ear for "sense by the yard," Gaskell, on one occasion apprised that the Martineaus were about to join her, confessed an impatience with the constraints of logic and duty. "I wish they weren't coming," she wrote. "I like to range about ad libitum, & sit out looking at views &c; not talking sense by the yard" (LG, 453/597, 163/239).

This is not to say that in her supernatural tales Gaskell flung sense to the wind to indulge in utter nonsense. On the contrary, the Victorian ghost story remained vested in reality as the women who wrote in this mode could still express themselves, though more luridly, about social

43. Mrs. Gaskell, 165.
44. Gypsy-Bachelor, 10, 111–12, and passim. Bonaparte's argument for Gaskell's drive to get back to the life of the demon weakens, if indeed it does not neutralize, the problematics of the witch image that Gaskell, I think, finally treats with marked ambivalence.

realities and conditions. Thus, Gaskell capitalized on the ghost story's intrinsic association with presence, absence, and power to look more closely at relations between women who, if not morbid, are dissatisfied, spiritually awry, or witched in some way. In Gaskell's supernatural tales the prevalence of the curse, the nature of which is to strip humans of all control over events, self, and others, underscores not only the idea of spiritual malaise but also the equivocal nature of women's powers.[45] In "The Poor Clare" when a heartsick Bridget Fitzgerald curses the man who has injured her, her powers are undercut by the fact that she has thereby cursed her granddaughter. As in the case of Eliot's Latimer, who finds that his gift of clairvoyant powers is really a curse, Bridget is caught between power and powerlessness.

With an emphasis on the human side of supernaturalism—curses and uncanny mental processes—Gaskell, like Eliot, presented the supernatural differently than did the Brontës with their nonhuman ghosts, preternatural storms, and disembodied voices. For Gaskell and Eliot in their shorter and more tentative stories, the line between the natural or rational and the supernatural is blurred, while for the Brontës there is no line, as the supernatural tends to be natural. Each writer used supernaturalism to different ends. For Charlotte Brontë the supernatural was a clearing in which she could confront the dire truths about otherness and self; for Emily Brontë it was part and parcel of her character's emancipation and fulfillment; for Eliot it was an opportunity to explore ambivalence; for Gaskell it was an appealing and dramatic means of looking more closely at women witched, as it were, in their relations and in their powers.

---

45. It is noteworthy that curses are not as common, nor characters quite as impotent, in the supernatural stories of Gaskell's and Eliot's male counterparts. By undoing his past evils, Dickens's Scrooge avoids a predetermined fate such as that which will engulf Gaskell's Furnivall. Bulwer Lytton's character in "The House and the Brain" seeks out the haunted house, goes in, pits his will against the supernaturally projected will of a dead malignant magician, and comes away the powerful victor. Bridget Fitzgerald, however, on confronting her grandchild's doppelgänger in "The Poor Clare" has nothing short of death and God's mercy to overcome the supernatural bane. The curse in supernatural stories appears to be a distinctly feminine phenomenon.

6

ANGELS, MONEY, AND GHOSTS
POPULAR VICTORIAN WOMEN
WRITERS OF THE SUPERNATURAL

CHARLOTTE AND Emily Brontë, George Eliot, and Elizabeth Gaskell had all published their ventures into the supernatural by 1859, the year of Darwin's *Origin of Species.* Darwin's work, as well as the writings of "The Seven against Christ" and Bishop Colenso, might be expected to have given primacy in the following years to the empirical spirit that had, from the start, challenged and qualified Victorian supernaturalism. But other female writers of lesser literary stature who had been writing numinous fiction, often anonymously for such journals as *All the Year Round* and *Belgravia,* would continue to flourish in the 1860s and 1870s. Indeed, Catherine Crowe, whose *Night Side of Nature* had been so popular in an earlier decade, published her *Ghosts and Family Legends* on Christmas of 1859, marking the end of a decade that had been significant in the history of the ghost story. Cox and Gilbert, who observe that the "art of the literary ghost story was perfected in the middle decades of the nineteenth century through the medium of magazines," have identified the 1850s as the period during which "the distinct, anti-Gothic character of the Victorian ghost story begins to emerge."[1] That is, it was during

---

1. Cox and Gilbert, eds. *Victorian Ghost Stories,* xi, x. For another discussion of the impact of the magazine on the ghost story, see Lynette Carpenter and Wendy K. Kolmar, eds., *Haunting the House*

this period that the Gothic formulation of the pure, innocent persecuted female, dependent on some male, usually an uncle who either owns or has appropriated her property and thus her financial and social power, began to be reversed.

The ghost stories written after the 1850s, but especially in the last decades of the century, would be written in a climate of change and reform marked by such developments as the agitation for women's rights to education, employment, and suffrage; the passage of the married women's property bills; and the rise of the New Woman. The pressure for change, which looked, to the alarm of the patriarchal society, like the feminization of the world, would bring about in the 1860s and in the 1890s the meteorlike advent of two literary forms that nonetheless reflected and helped create "a changing feminine mythology"—the sensation novel and the writings of the New Woman. After the 1850s, the supernatural story would share the scene with the sensation novel, which in its focus on such subjects as bigamy, adultery, and female eroticism would anticipate the second bedfellow of the supernatural tale, the writing of the New Woman, with its emphasis on sexual and social liberation and its critique of marriage. The supernatural story would not be unaffected by what Lyn Pykett, in her excellent comparative study of the women's sensation novel and New Woman writing, terms the "improper feminine."[2]

In ascendancy after 1859,[3] the sensation novel appealed to a readership quite similar to that which had welcomed the earlier incursions into the supernatural. In fact, Victorians themselves may well have characterized supernaturalism as sensational fiction since, as P. D. Edwards points out, " 'sensation novel' is a popular generic term, usually disparaging, for crime, mystery, and horror novels."[4] In its mixture of melodrama and "scientific" verisimilitude, the fiction of sensation simultaneously

---

of Fiction: Feminist Perspectives on Ghost Stories by American Women, 6–7. In their introduction, Carpenter and Kolmar, who argue for an American women's ghost story tradition, also note more generally "the existence of a distinctive women's tradition of ghost story writing in both England and the U.S. from 1850 on" (10).

2. I borrow the phrase "a changing feminine mythology" from Patricia Marks's *Bicycles, Bangs, and Bloomers: The New Woman in the Popular Press*, 2; Pykett, *The "Improper" Feminine: The Women's Sensation Novel and the New Woman Writing*.

3. Winifred Hughes, *The Maniac in the Cellar: Sensation Novels of the 1860's*, 3–15.

4. "Sensation Novel," in Mitchell, ed., *Victorian Britain: An Encyclopedia*, 703.

placated the opposing appetites for escapism and "fact" that also no doubt characterized earlier readers. Yet far from displacing the taste for supernatural fiction, the cult of sensation in the 1860s only seems to have made it sharper. The sensation novel never succeeded in wholly eclipsing its rival. Bulwer Lytton published his supernatural *Strange Story* in 1862; Sheridan Le Fanu published "Squire Toby's Will" in 1868 and his redoubtable "Green Tea" in 1869. *All the Year Round*, which Dickens edited until his death in 1870, ran not only Bulwer's *Strange Story* and several pieces by Le Fanu as well as Dickens's own ghost story "The Signalman" (1866) but also Rosa Mulholland's "Not to Be Taken at Bed-time" (1865) and some of Amelia B. Edwards's best-known supernatural tales: "The Four-Fifteen Express," "My Brother's Ghost Story," "How the Third Floor Knew the Potteries," "The Phantom Coach," and "The Engineer," nearly all of which first appeared in Dickens's journal during the 1860s.[5] Rhoda Broughton would publish her story "The Truth, the Whole Truth, and Nothing but the Truth" in 1868, while Mrs. Henry Wood's "Reality or Delusion?" would also be published that same year.

The last quarter of the nineteenth century is particularly rich in supernatural tales by men including Robert Louis Stevenson, Bram Stoker, Thomas Hardy, and Oscar Wilde and, what is more to the point, by women including Mary Elizabeth Braddon, Amelia B. Edwards, Mary Louisa Molesworth, and Rosa Mulholland. This period is also specifically notable as "the single era in human history when a serious, systematic attempt was made to census the supernatural" through such agencies as the Society for Psychical Research in Britain and the American Society for Psychical Research.[6] As studies such as Ann Braude's *Radical Spirits: Spiritualism and Women's Rights in Nineteenth-Century America*, Alex Owen's *The Darkened Room: Women, Power and Spiritualism in Late Victorian England*, and Diana Basham's *The Trial of Woman: Feminism and the Occult Sciences in Victorian Literature and Society* have demonstrated, developments in the supernatural revival of the nineteenth century, such as the founding of the Society for Psychical Research, influenced other sociopolitical movements involving women, especially suffrage and early feminism.

5. Other supernatural titles published in *All the Year Round* during this period are "Ghost Stories," "An Old Spirit Medium," "Ghost Raising," and "Spectres."

6. E. F. Bleiler, introduction to *The Collected Ghost Stories of Mrs. J. H. Riddell*, ed. Bleiler, xviii.

Unlike the supernatural tale, the sensation novel usually relied not on apparitions or curses but on murder, seduction, and bigamy. As Margaret Oliphant says of Wilkie Collins's sensational *Woman in White* (1860), there was "no desire to tinge the daylight with any morbid shadows . . . effects are produced by common human acts performed by recognisable human agents." The sensation novel deals more with shocks and thrills of this world than with a fear of the inexplicable and otherworldly as it tends boldly to subvert Victorian prudery and morality. Still, like the ghost story, this special child of the 1860s represented an attempt "to get some grandeur and sacredness restored to life—or if not sacredness and grandeur, at least horror and mystery." But while supernaturalism remained comparatively wary and conservative in its reaction to the Victorian era's massive spiritual and material changes, the sensation novel, with its presumably "female, middle-class, and leisured" audience, reacted to these changes with radical zest.[7]

It is significant that Eliza Linton, who was to become a severe critic of the sensation novel and subsequently of the New Woman, should have earlier shown her similar disapproval of the supernatural: in 1861, two years after the publication of Crowe's veracious collection, *Ghosts and Family Legends,* Linton's own collection of reportedly factual witch stories was meant to point out "the fraud and deceit flung over every such account" as well as "the likeness between these stories and the marvels going on now in modern society." In her later disparagement of the fiction of sensation, Linton, despite the example of Wilkie Collins, regarded the form as a distinctly feminine phenomenon: "What man would dare to write like 'Ouida?' and who but women have founded, and continued, and to this hour uphold the sensationalist school?"[8]

Indeed, for writers such as M. E. Braddon, Rhoda Broughton, "Ouida," and Mrs. Henry Wood, the sensational novel appears to have acted as a bolder vehicle of a feminine desire for more freedom and action than did the supernatural tale. Whereas supernatural stories by female writers tend to evince a more subtle exploration of the feminine condition—whether in the isolation of the moors or in the thick of the materialistic industrial city—sensation novels give voice to a distinct and

7. [Oliphant,] "Sensation Novels," 566, 565; Elaine Showalter, *A Literature of Their Own: British Women Novelists from Brontë to Lessing,* 159.

8. Linton, ed., *Witch Stories,* 106; Linton, *Ourselves,* 185.

brazen protest against woman's place. Elaine Showalter contends that this peculiar genre, with its secrets,

> made crime and violence domestic, modern, and suburban; but their secrets were not simply solutions to mysteries and crimes; they were the secrets of women's dislike of their roles as daughters, wives, and mothers. These women novelists made a powerful appeal to the female audience by subverting the traditions of feminine fiction to suit their own imaginative impulses, by expressing a wide range of suppressed female emotions, and by tapping and satisfying fantasies of protest and escape. . . . Sensation novels expressed female anger, frustration, and sexual energy more directly than had been done previously.[9]

These novels of passionate crime, sex, and violence served their purpose for a while, but the form could finally not survive long in Victorian England because, among other things, it was itself too blatantly the antithesis of Victorianism. Even Braddon and Wood tended to succumb to the spirit of the age and punish their heroines: the sensation novelists "used" this "transitional literature" to explore "genuinely radical female protest against marriage and women's economic oppression, although still in the framework of feminine conventions that demanded the erring heroine's destruction." By the mid-1870s, the sensation novel as a distinct genre had passed away, while the supernatural tale fully reasserted itself as a popular form during the 1870s and 1880s, again by the 1890s not only making room for but also adopting some of the sensationalism of yet another *écriture féminine* about the New Woman that inscribed women's "inexorable [move] away from a stereotype that bound them to domestic concerns."[10] If the sensation novel had worked as an emetic, the supernatural story had the effect of a slower, but steadier tonic. For writers Margaret Oliphant (1828–1897), Charlotte Riddell (1832–1906), and Florence Marryat (1838–1899), considered below, it would continue to act as a medium for powerful female "fantasies of protest and escape."

Even for Charlotte Brontë and George Eliot, the ghost story's potential as a safety valve for the age and as a vehicle for questioning identity and roles had not been its only enticement. As Miriam Allot's comments about Gaskell's short stories suggest, though somewhat simplistically

---

9. *A Literature of Their Own,* 158–60.

10. Ibid., 28–29; Marks, *Bicycles, Bangs, and Bloomers,* ix. See Lyn Pykett on the relation of *l'écriture féminine* to the sensation novel and New Woman writing in *"Improper" Feminine,* 169–71, 206–9.

and reductively, "they succeeded in their chief purpose—to keep the pot boiling and provide a Victorian lady with pin-money." Money undoubtedly drew men and women writers to the supernatural story, but near the end of the century the money women earned from the sale of such stories would be significant both as a means of acquiring independence and as a means of obtaining a living, not just as pin money. Ghost stories were a highly marketable item, especially around Christmas, a holiday that, with its mystical associations, encouraged a suspension of disbelief.[11] Publishing their tales during the latter part of the nineteenth century, Oliphant, Riddell, and Marryat—popular female writers who probed the nature of woman's special relation to the spiritual and the material, which often meant money—were in fact earning their own bread at a time when women were more openly challenging ideas of female submissiveness and economic powerlessness.

During the last half of the nineteenth century a movement was afoot to raise the status of the Victorian female, who was for all intents and purposes politically and economically a slave, if not indeed "civilly dead." Women such as Barbara Leigh Smith Bodichon, who deplored the condition of coverture whereby a woman's "existence is entirely absorbed in that of her husband," would agitate for the right to own property. In *The Subjection of Women,* John Stuart Mill proposed that the wife denied the privilege of being a property holder "is the actual bond-servant of her husband: no less so, as far as legal obligation goes, than slaves commonly so called. . . . She can acquire no property but for him; the instant it becomes hers, even if by inheritance, it becomes *ipso facto* his."[12]

This neo-Gothic condition would finally be mitigated by the married women's property law.[13] However, married women were not the

11. Allott, *Elizabeth Gaskell,* 12. Many ghost stories appeared in Christmas annuals. As the author of *A Christmas Carol, The Chimes,* and *The Haunted Man,* and as the editor of *Household Words* and *All the Year Round,* Charles Dickens helped establish the ghost story as a Christmas staple. In *Private Theatricals* Auerbach comments, "In Victorian England, Christmas was ghost season. A ritualistic culture, yearning feverishly for transcendence, possessed by faith but deprived of dogma, turned the occasion of the Savior's birth into a festival of weird apparitions" (102).

12. "The Seneca Falls Declaration," in Erna Olafson Hellerstein, Leslie Parker Hume, and Karen M. Offen, eds., *Victorian Women: A Documentary Account of Women's Lives in Nineteenth-Century England, France, and the United States,* 165; "Barbara Leigh Smith Bodichon," in Hellerstein, Hume, and Offen, eds., *Victorian Women: A Documentary Account,* 164; Mill, *The Subjection of Women,* 31.

13. It is interesting that, as Lee Holcombe argues in *Wives and Property: Reform of the Married Women's Property Law in Nineteenth-Century England,* the reform of women's property laws came

only women to experience economic oppression, as the single woman, spinster or widow, knew not only economic disadvantage but also social castigation that is mirrored in the descriptions of her as "redundant," "superfluous," "superabundant," and "supernumerary." Without husbands, these women were dependent on uncles, brothers, and cousins. Put in the uncomfortable position of being extras and economic burdens, it is no wonder that "at the end of the century" the "increasing number of women [who] failed to fulfill traditional expectations to marry and to rear children" rose up and came to wish for "all the advantages of their brothers . . . education, suffrage, and careers."[14]

Linton, who unlike Mill decried the "uprising" of females, described with great misgivings the revolt of the modern woman in a series of articles first published in the *Saturday Review* and later collected under the title *The Girl of the Period*. Of the man and woman of the period Linton wrote in spite of herself with seeming sympathy: "She is but a servant to him; an honoured servant, if you will, but a servant all the same; and while she has not the means of self-support she can be nothing else, and must show herself obedient if she would be grateful. . . . This is the real meaning of the modern revolt—women want to be independent, and to be on terms of monetary equality with men."[15] Money not only put food on the table, it also empowered.

Unsurprisingly, Oliphant, Marryat, and especially Riddell, raising specters of restitution and revenge, wrote supernatural tales strongly preoccupied with money and murders committed for that money. This preoccupation with money is not usually so blatant in the tales of earlier major women authors. Far more than money, Emily Brontë's Heathcliff desires revenge and the status that money may bring him in order to have Catherine; though he ultimately causes Catherine's death, he is hardly her murderer. Like Jane Eyre, the characters in Gaskell's supernatural stories reveal little in the way of greed, for they are either born with money and position, as are Miss Furnivall in "The Old Nurse's Story" and Owen Griffiths in "The Doom of the Griffiths," or, like Bridget Fitzgerald in "The Poor Clare," they are satisfied with what they have.

---

about mostly because of economic conditions, not because of the arguments that were being made in favor of reform (8).

14. Marks, *Bicycles, Bangs, and Bloomers*, 24, 2.

15. Linton, *Ourselves*, 227–28.

Even in Eliot's *The Lifted Veil*, where Bertha murders Mrs. Archer and plans to kill Latimer, money is not the issue; the couple is, after all, "surrounded by all the appliances of wealth" (*Veil*, 46). In Riddell's "The Open Door" (1882), however, a woman who has stabbed her husband to death returns to the haunted Ladlow Hall to search for a will that would deprive her of money. When a clerk who is venturing to solve the mystery of the haunted house surprises the woman, she fights like a wild cat, biting, kicking, and scratching. The clerk recalls that the woman "had the strength of twenty devils . . . and struggled as surely no woman ever did before."[16] In this story, which represents, along with the sensation novel and New Woman writing, what Pykett calls the "transgressive" female who is neither passive, nor nurturing, nor the linchpin of marriage,[17] the focus is not so much on the spiritual condition of the character as on that character's preoccupation with the disposition of the material. The desire for money has transformed the demure angel into a fury the male can barely control: "She turned and twisted and slipped about like a snake, but I did not feel pain or anything except a deadly horror lest my strength should give out" ("Open," 66).

Because Riddell was a novelist of the London business world, it is only natural that a greater proportion of her ghost stories dwell on the power of materialism and financial knowledge. Her insistence on sovereigns, trade, warehouses, creditors, debts, and properties gives her stories a matter-of-factness that enhances their realism. When the materialism of her stories begins to fade into the surrealism of the ghostly, the junction can lead to such passages as the following from "Nut Bush Farm" (published, like Oliphant's "Open Door," the year of the Married Women's Property Act of 1882), in which shrewd Miss Gostock sells a farm to the male protagonist:

> Like one in a dream I sat and watched Miss Gostock while she wrote. Nothing about the transaction seemed to me real. The farm itself resembled nothing I had ever before seen with my waking eyes, and Miss Gostock appeared to me but as some monstrous figure in a story of giants and hobgoblins. The man's coat, the woman's skirt, the hobnailed shoes, the grisly hair, the old straw hat, the bare, unfurnished room, the

16. "The Open Door," in *The Collected Ghost Stories of Mrs. J. H. Riddell*, ed. Bleiler, 66; hereafter cited parenthetically as "Open."

17. *"Improper" Feminine*, 9–10.

bright sunshine outside, all struck me as mere accessories in a play—as nothing which had any hold on the outside, everyday world.[18]

Words and phrases like "dream," "monstrous," "giants and goblins" help cast an air of ghostly twilight over the harsh material reality created by the writing, the "transaction, the hobnailed shoes," and "bright sunshine." The male character tries to contain the economic power of the propertied female by insisting on the spectralness of the business deal: it is a dream or a play in which the woman figures as one grisly and monstrous. Presenting the woman here as a ghostly being, the male protagonist acknowledges her power while he seeks to undercut it. Interestingly enough, the real ghost that finally does materialize is a man notably materialistic even in death as he stalks the Beach Walk in his Palmerston suit and round hat, with his light cane and diamond ring. Yet Riddell's stories for all their materialism are usually qualified by the ghost, an often sympathetic figure.

In tales such as *The Uninhabited House*, published in 1875, and "The Old House in Vauxhall Walk" and "Walnut-Tree House," both published in 1882, Riddell continues to mix the spiritual and the financial. In these tales, Riddell, who tends to be very much aware of the house as a financial asset or a piece of property, investigates the relationship of domesticity to money. The rare *Uninhabited House* concerns the fortunes of one irascible and shrewd Miss Blake and her niece Helena Elmsdale. The two women flee River Hall, a comfortable and modern house, the gaslights of which seem to exclude the possibility of its being "ghost-ridden,"[19] when they find that the house is indeed haunted. Although they are physically free of the house, Miss Blake and her niece are economically trapped by it: the women depend on the income the house brings when it is let. Because it is haunted by the ghost of Helena's father, who ironically wants to restore his daughter to wealth, the house does not bring much money. Consequently, outside the house and thus outside the domestic sphere, the women have a hard time supporting themselves. In this tale, then, Riddell has not only made the habitat of the angel in the house uninhabitable, but she has also suggested how the woman who is bound to hearth and home may be financially disadvantaged. It is only when

18. "Nut Bush Farm," in *Collected Ghost Stories*, 9.
19. *The Uninhabited House*, 20; hereafter cited parenthetically as *Uninhabited*.

the ghost reveals the mystery of River Hall that Helena becomes an heiress, a "pretty autocrat" (*Uninhabited,* 111) who has the power to establish her own hearth on her own terms and who has the boldness to propose marriage to a young office clerk who is socially and financially beneath her.

In "The Old House in Vauxhall Walk" and "Walnut-Tree House," amid the rich appointments of handsome homes, there is poverty for the old woman and young child who figure, respectively, in the two stories. Although she lives in a "fine house" of "magnificent proportions" that "still spoke mutely of the wealth and stability of the original owner," old Miss Tynan suffers a poverty of person and spirit.[20] Her miserly love of sovereigns transforms her into one "filthy of person, repulsive to look at, hard of heart" ("Old House," 93). She is no one's angel; she is at the center of no one's hearth. "Her heart was as invulnerable to natural affection as it had proved to human sympathy. . . . She was solitary in a desolate house, with a deeper blackness than the darkness of night waiting to engulf her" ("Old House," 93). After two men murder Miss Tynan for her money, she returns to the old house repentant and painfully anxious to leave her hidden hoard to the family she had mistreated in life. The money she eventually reveals to her heirs becomes her own as well as her kinsfolk's salvation.

In "Walnut-Tree House," Edgar Stainton finds the house he has inherited haunted by the ghost of a child "poorly dressed, wasted and worn."[21] Starved and harshly treated by his guardian, the young boy had died when his sister had gone to live with another relative. Acquiring what Auerbach calls "the intensified power of the dead," the boy had a "vulnerability" that "enhanc[ed his] spectacular power";[22] twelve years later, he has taken possession of the property and has "driven tenant after tenant out of the premises" ("Walnut-Tree," 158). The little ghost is not laid to rest until a will is disclosed that in effect restores the boy's sister to the hearth of Walnut-Tree House. "She was found; the lost had come again to meet a living friend on the once desolate hearth. . . . She

20. "The Old House in Vauxhall Walk," in *Collected Ghost Stories,* 88, 87; hereafter cited parenthetically as "Old House."

21. "Walnut-Tree House," in *Collected Ghost Stories,* 156; hereafter cited parenthetically as "Walnut-Tree."

22. *Private Theatricals,* 44.

was come! Through years he had kept faithful watch for her, but the waiting was ended now" ("Walnut-Tree," 170).

Similar fantasies of restoration underlie the works of Oliphant and Marryat. In the former's "Old Lady Mary," the ghost of the title character seeks to bestow all her earthly goods on the young lady who is her ward. In her endeavor, the old woman affords some insight into female power and powerlessness. As an independent and rich old lady, Mary has power and contentment, but when she dies and makes her debut as a ghost, she discovers a sad truth about the angel in the house. For, as a ghost, old Lady Mary should wield great powers. But just as Eliot in *The Lifted Veil* undercuts Latimer's preternatural powers by making them a bane, and just as Gaskell in "The Poor Clare" punishes Bridget Fitzgerald for her supernaturally retributive powers, so Oliphant seems to undercut "the power of [Lady Mary's] new faculties."[23] Although a spirit she may be, she is still a woman, and "she began to weep, in the terrible failure and contrariety of all things but yet she would not yield" ("Old Lady," 124–25). The longing for power surfaces in the supernatural story, but in compliance with the dictates of society it is quickly if not completely put down. Instead, while woman's strength and will are cautiously revealed, woman's power of sympathy and her capacity for suffering are openly glorified. The ghost of Lady Mary returns to earth in order to disclose a testament she has perversely hidden, a testament that will save the old lady's namesake from poverty. But in the struggle to champion the values of justice, charity, and pity, woman (in the form of the ghost of old Lady Mary) is neither heard nor seen except by the little girl Connie, by an innocent baby—woman's special province—and by a dog. Consequently Mary is helpless. "She could do nothing then—nothing" ("Old Lady," 154).

Elsewhere in the story the ghost of the old lady observes how hard it is "to be thus left outside of life, to speak and not be heard, to stand, unseen, astounded, unable to secure any attention" ("Old Lady," 145). The author wishes the reader to sympathize with this invisibility, voice-lessness, and helplessness that may well have constituted a significant part of the experience of many Victorian women who were less literally

---

23. "Old Lady Mary," in *Two Stories of the Seen and the Unseen,* 154; hereafter cited parenthetically as "Old Lady."

angels in the house. Clearly, Oliphant identified with her protagonist, as she herself once wrote: "Sometimes I am miserable—always there is in me . . . the gnawing pangs of anxiety, and deep, deep dissatisfaction beyond words, and the sense of helplessness, which of itself is despair." In working out the answers to her life, to her financial difficulties, and to her bouts of feminine despair in her supernatural tales, Oliphant, who was no advocate of the New Woman and who was in fact the most conservative of the popular writers here considered, felt a comfort that was particularly necessary to her as a vessel of woe, a woman. "Here is the end of all," she wrote at a time of sorrow in 1864, "I am alone, I am a woman." And again she wrote, "I have had all the usual experiences of woman, never impressing anybody,—what a droll little complaint!—why should I?"[24]

Oddly and significantly, though the ghost of Old Lady Mary never impresses the doctor, lawyer, or vicar, she does impress her ward, Miss Vivian; Mrs. Bowyer, the vicar's wife; and Connie's mother, Mrs. Turner —the women and the children. Old Lady Mary's powers are, thus, qualified. The women as opposed to the more worldly men prove either more receptive or more credulous of the supernatural. They are thus mythically reaffirmed as the more spiritual beings even as they are psychologically criticized for gullibility. Their strength may also be perceived as a weakness; women are once again deprived of an unequivocal triumph. Oddly, Lady Mary is not even directly responsible for the financial restoration of her ward, but she does return to the kingdom of spirits in some way wiser, uplifted, glorified. " 'I am forgiven' she said, with a low cry of happiness. 'She whom I wronged, loves me and blessed me' " ("Old Lady," 212).

Money is of obvious importance in Marryat's lurid *The Strange Transformation of Hannah Stubbs* (1896). Here the spirit of the unfaithful Marchesa de Sorrento, murdered by her husband in a jealous rage, possesses the servant girl Hannah, whom the Marchese has married, and compels her to kill her husband in order to gain the wealth and power a richer suitor would confer on her. In Marryat's supernatural novel, the angel in the house has become a demon hell-bent on getting money. Marryat's Marchesa de Sorrento, who could have been the heroine of

---

24. *Autobiography and Letters of Mrs. Margaret Oliphant*, 4, 94, 8.

a sensation novel, bodies forth the later Victorian woman's struggle for visibility and independence. Again it was the sharply critical Linton who noted that the "modern" woman of the later nineteenth century was a woman characterized by an "impatience . . . and a restless ambition to do something of a more active and notorious kind than the domestic duties assigned to her for her portion." This discontent with her lot led the modern woman to "an inordinate desire for money, because of the social influence and excitement it can command."[25] Conceivably, for writers like Marryat, the new emphasis on murder and money became the prime means of expressing the yearning for the action and freedom of movement for which the New Woman, that "determined figure in bloomers," would campaign when she "cut [her] hair, adopted 'rational' dress, and freewheeled along a path that led to the twentieth century."[26] Murder is certainly a radical defiance of the domestic duties deemed to be the proper sphere for female action; and money, as I have already suggested, is clearly perceived as a mark of independence.

While the female supernaturalist certainly had no exclusive claim on the theme of money and murder in ghost stories, the persistence of the concern in the supernatural tales of women points us in some telling directions. The themes of money and murder, power and independence are not far afield of exploitation and revenge. If the Victorian woman was awakening to the power of the pound sterling, she was also discovering the satisfaction of aggression and revenge that entailed "women's use of their intransigent powers" to address "a perceived wrong committed against them or against their loved ones."[27]

One striking figure in the works of Riddell and Marryat, for instance, is the lone and vengeful female ghost. Both the little female ghost in Gaskell's "The Old Nurse's Story" and Catherine's ghost in *Wuthering Heights* beg with unnerving persistence to come in out of the cold, but though they are just as persevering, the female ghosts found in the stories by later writers are not only older but also less humble and more aggressive than their predecessors. Old Mrs. Jones, in Riddell's tale by that name, stops at nothing within the power of the dead to avenge

25. Linton, *Ourselves*, 240.

26. Marks, *Bicycles, Bangs, and Bloomers*, 2.

27. In "Writing as Voodoo," Barreca also notes "the uncanny methods women use to secure their own ends," one of which is revenge (187).

herself on her greedy young murderous husband, while in "A Terrible Vengeance" (1889) a younger and lovelier woman than old Mrs. Jones, jilted and drowned by her lover, returns and doggedly pursues him, then literally stamps him to death with her tiny wet footprints. As Regina Barreca, writing about women's power and magic puts it, "Denied love, [these women] choose death as their vocation. Denied access to those areas of knowledge considered credible, they will deal with the incredible."[28]

Marryat, too, portrays unladylike, forceful, almost combative female ghosts. We have seen how Marchesa de Sorrento exacts her revenge through Hannah Stubbs. What remains to be seen is how the males in the story use the female. When the two men in the tale stumble upon the homely country servant Hannah, they discover that she is an excellent materializing medium. The first of these men, the Marchese, wants to get in contact with the wife he has murdered; the second wishes to learn what he can about spirits for the edification of mankind. Without any regard for the welfare of Hannah, the first man so frequently uses the servant's powers to communicate with his wife that the wife's evil spirit possesses the girl's body. Although the spirit eventually decamps, the girl herself dies.

Like the angel in the house, Hannah has powers that are for the benefit of the male. Unsurprisingly, she is exploited by a man who perverts her powers for his own selfish purposes. But the male cannot exploit the vengeful demonic woman who becomes, as it were, Hannah's other self. In what may be termed her spiritualistic manifesto, *The Spirit World,* Marryat indirectly sheds some light on Hannah Stubbs when she encourages her readers at every turn to "know everything" and to "judge for ourselves" before they can assume control of their own lives. For Marryat, who alleged that she herself was a medium, one had to be strong and autonomous before one could experience spiritualism as the "unmitigated blessing" she knew it to be. It is not unfair to suppose that Marryat found the same strength and autonomy necessary to be a Victorian woman.

Although *Hannah Stubbs* is one of Marryat's most sensational supernatural pieces, one of the most charming yet chilling portraits of

28. Ibid., 189.

feminine persistence, aggression, and revenge appears in "The Ghost of Charlotte Cray." Miss Cray is a middle-aged authoress whom the forty-year-old publisher Sigismund Braggett finds a financial risk, but nonetheless an exceedingly clever woman to have around the firm. In the meantime, Sigismund allows Miss Cray to think that he loves her. Needless to say, when Sigismund marries a pretty young lady named Emily, Miss Cray, emotionally and professionally exploited, is not happy. Consequently, she visits Sigismund's office, leaves him notes, and posts letters to him threatening that she will not desist until he introduces her to his wife. At first, Sigismund is annoyed, but when Miss Cray's visits and letters suddenly cease he becomes concerned and visits her house, only to find that she has been dead for a week. It is a bloodcurdling shock, then, when Miss Cray's notes, letters, and, yes, even her visits start again. Her determination to see the pretty young Mrs. Braggett lives beyond the grave, and she haunts Sigismund relentlessly until she accomplishes a meeting with Emily.

The female ghosts in these two stories body forth the energies of liberated, even if somewhat negatively liberated, woman. The female shades in "The Terrible Vengeance" and in "Charlotte Cray" aggressively wield their powers of revenge. In *Wuthering Heights,* it is the civilized Lockwood who brutally attacks the pleading apparition in his dream; in the ghost stories of Riddell, Oliphant, and Marryat, the specters of the dead (female as well as male) are given powers of revenge that clearly mirror their creators' own desires to avenge a keenly felt deprivation, especially when that deprivation is financial. There is a strong identification both with the victimization that leads to the ghost's unrest as well as with the restitutions the ghost makes possible. Recall Riddell's female Scrooge who haunts the old Vauxhall dwelling until her murderers are ruined and her hoard of money is given to her heir. "Money can't bring back the dead to life" ("Walnut-Tree," 164), says another of Riddell's characters. But by animating ghosts who punish thieves and murderers—and, what is more, by profiting from such writing—Riddell disproved this statement in a paradox that constitutes a necessary strategy for coping with oppression.

If the impression of vengeful ghosts suggests a less disguised treatment of resentments that the earlier writers had concealed or not felt, the more conspicuous preoccupation with the acquisition of money suggests a greater self-consciousness on the part of women writers who had become the breadwinners for their families and themselves. Charlotte Brontë may have helped support her father's household with her writing and teaching, Gaskell secretly bought her husband a house, and Eliot's authorship insured an income for Lewes and his sons. Yet for the new generation of writers, authorship had come to mean financial independence, a token of liberated energies as well as a means of survival.

This is not to say that the popular writers were hard materialists or devotees of mammon. Oliphant, for example, in her long supernatural work *The Beleaguered City* (1880) has spirits rise up and chastise the male citizens of Semur who say that money is God. Riddell piously insists in her short stories that money is the root of all evil. Yet, on another level, money in the supernatural tales becomes the source of well-being for deprived widows, children, and descendants to whom it rightfully belongs, just as in real life it had become a means to the well-being and security that women had once been able to acquire only through marriage. Money would be a step toward equality, an economic equality of which these popular female authors especially knew the value, just as surely as the supernatural was a step for nineteenth-century British women toward the release of pent-up feminine energies.

The pen in the hands of these women writing the supernatural was less a "metaphorical penis," to borrow Gilbert and Gubar's expression,[29] than a wand of visibility. Writing a ghost story or for that matter an essay calling for the investigation of ghosts had for the nineteenth-century woman the double meaning not only of making out of the nothingness of the white page something visible (metaphorically the very act of writing is ghostly) but also of making her position as well as her self legible, visible, readable, so that she who had been legally, financially, even intellectually absent in the broad light of day could assert in her supernatural writings the truth of her spiritual and cultural being.

29. *Madwoman in the Attic,* 3.

Conclusion

FROM THE vantage point of the end of the twentieth century, the supernaturalism of earlier ages may appear even more a matter of fear, superstition, and ignorance; however, the persistence of supernaturalism in so-called enlightened and scientific times such as the Victorian period as well as our own signifies deeply about meaning and knowledge, experience and being. The persistence of the supernatural, for instance, says something about the nature of meaning itself because it testifies to an alternative knowledge that in the end is necessary to the existence of categorical knowledge. As Theodor Adorno, writing about the essay—a form that has itself been, like the supernatural story, "classified as a trivial endeavor"—puts it: "the objective wealth of meanings encapsulated in every intellectual phenomenon demands of the recipient the same spontaneity of subjective fantasy that is castigated in the name of objective discipline." In other words, there can be no light without darkness, no flesh without spirit. The query then is not that which Cruikshank and others have set forth—"Cui bono"—or what good is all this talk of ghosts? The query is what does it all mean? Once this question is posed, we come closer, as Daniel Cottom in *Abyss of Reason* astutely observes, to acknowledging "that the issue of empirical verification has no necessary precedence over the issue of meaning, which may actually constitute a telling critique of the tendency to identify empiricism with truth."[1] The supernatural makes room for that "spontaneity of subjective fantasy" that can in turn open up an "objective wealth of meanings." The supernatural idea, but especially the supernatural tale, allows for play, speculation, investigation, and redefinition.

Since science, technology, and reason have no more exorcised the ghosts of Emily Brontë's *Wuthering Heights* than they have the ghost of Toni Morrison's *Beloved*, reason or realism, as Cottom argues, "could not help but see," in a movement like spiritualism, "its own troubling, earnest, mocking [even playful, I would add] double," and recognize that double most strikingly inscribed in supernatural stories, especially stories about ghosts. The notion of the double brings us to another and, for the purposes of this study, more telling way in which the supernatural or ghost story signifies: it provides a preserve for the other, countering that "tendency to deny centrality to any experience that [does] not conform to the world of reason."[2] As such it speaks subtly, though powerfully and most particularly, to the life and experience of the Victorian woman who was socially, biologically, and culturally cast as other, as second, as the unscientific and the nonintellectual one, not the real or most substantial thing as beings go in either a hierarchical society or a dichotomized democracy.

In *Private Theatricals*, Nina Auerbach sheds light on women, ghosts, and the other via the kind of definition and play that occurs on the theatrical stage when she remarks that, for the Victorians, "Actors and ghosts both appear as unnatural impositions on authentic being. But underneath their assurance that they know who they are, Victorian humanists fear that the disobedient energies of the actor and the ghost manifest truer, if trickier, 'own selves' than the authorized cycle of life accommodates."[3] Although Auerbach was writing about the stage or theatricality, her equation of ghosts with disobedient energies and truer selves is doubly significant for women whose "authorized" roles required a spirituality predicated on obedience and silence that kept them at a remove from the real world. Victorians could not but be concerned about

1. Adorno, "The Essay as Form," 4; Cottom, *Abyss of Reason*, 13.
2. Cottom, *Abyss of Reason*, 93, 20.
3. *Private Theatricals*, 18.

the authenticity of women who, for instance, brought themselves center stage as mediums at séances.

This book is in a sense about the theater of women's lives. It is neither a history of the supernatural nor a study of the rise of the ghost story. What I have done is discover the meanings found in and generated by the supernaturalism of nineteenth-century British women, especially the writers of fiction. One of the most important aims of this study has been to determine the ramifications of women connecting with the unsanctioned supernaturalism of séance, mesmerism, and ghosts. That intersection reveals that the supernatural illuminated, if it did not indeed endorse, the lives of some Victorian women. As for the women who wrote stories about ghosts, they themselves perceived through the experiences of their often female protagonists how ghosts stood, as Auerbach asserts, "in a tantalizing relation to the ideal of the own self."[4] As such, the supernaturalism of the nineteenth-century British woman writer constitutes an interesting spiritual bildungsroman about woman's desire and struggle to come to terms with her invisibility and visibility, with her essential in-betweenness, with her condition as a ghost in the noontide. Although it was not the room twentieth-century writer Virginia Woolf later declared one of the necessities for a woman writing fiction, the ghost story afforded some women a special space. The supernatural meant opportunity—the opportunity to indulge in a medium that seemed intrinsically to replicate the often disabling dichotomies that informed female culture, the opportunity not only to gain a better understanding of those dichotomies and the uses to which they could and could not be put but also to know better the nature of female experience and the feminine self.

4. Ibid.

Bibliography

Abrams, M. H. *Natural Supernaturalism: Tradition and Revolution in Romantic Literature.* New York: Norton, 1971.

Adorno, Theodor W. "The Essay as Form." In *Notes to Literature,* edited by Rolf Tiedemann, 1:3–36. New York: Columbia University Press, 1991.

Alaya, Flavia. "Victorian Science and the 'Genius' of Woman." *Journal of the History of Ideas* 38 (1977): 261–80.

Allott, Miriam. *Elizabeth Gaskell.* London: Longman, Green, and Co., 1960.

Armstrong, Nancy. *Desire and Domestic Fiction: A Political History of the Novel.* New York: Oxford University Press, 1987.

Arnold, Matthew. *Poetry and Criticism of Matthew Arnold.* Edited by Dwight Culler. Boston: Houghton Mifflin, 1961.

Ashley, Michael, ed. *Mrs Gaskell's Tales of Mystery and Horror.* London: Victor Gollancz, 1978.

Auerbach, Nina. *Private Theatricals: The Lives of the Victorians.* Cambridge: Harvard University Press, 1990.

———. *Woman and the Demon: The Life of a Victorian Myth.* Cambridge: Harvard University Press, 1982.

Baker, Augusta, and Ellin Greene. *Storytelling: Art and Technique.* New York: R. R. Bowker, 1977.

Barreca, Regina, ed. *Sex and Death in Victorian Literature.* Bloomington: Indiana University Press, 1990.

———. "Writing as Voodoo: Sorcery, Hysteria, and Art." In *Death and Representation,* edited by Elisabeth Bronfen and Sarah Webster Goodwin, 174–91. Baltimore: Johns Hopkins University Press, 1993.

Basham, Diana. *The Trial of Woman: Feminism and the Occult Sciences in Victorian Literature and Society.* Washington Square: New York University Press, 1992.

Bellringer, Alan W. *George Eliot.* New York: St. Martin's Press, 1993.

Bennett, Gillian. *Traditions of Belief: Women and the Supernatural.* London: Penguin, 1987.

Black, Helen. *Notable Women Authors of the Day.* London: Maclaren, 1906.

Bloom, Harold, ed. *The Brontës.* New York: Chelsea House, 1987.

Bonaparte, Felicia. *The Gypsy-Bachelor of Manchester: The Life of Mrs. Gaskell's Demon.* Charlottesville: University Press of Virginia, 1992.

———. *The Triptych and the Cross: The Central Myths of George Eliot's Poetic Imagination.* New York: New York University Press, 1979.

Boumelha, Penny. *Charlotte Brontë.* Bloomington: Indiana University Press, 1990.

Brantlinger, Patrick. *The Spirit of Reform: British Literature and Politics, 1832–1867.* Cambridge: Harvard University Press, 1977.

Braude, Ann. *Radical Spirits: Spiritualism and Women's Rights in Nineteenth-Century America.* Boston: Beacon Press, 1989.

Bray, Charles. *Phases of Opinion and Experience during a Long Life: An Autobiography.* London: Longmans, Green and Co., 1884.

———. *The Philosophy of Necessity.* 2 vols. London: Longman, Orme, Brown, Green, and Longmans, 1841.

Briggs, Julia. *Night Visitors: The Rise and Fall of the English Ghost Story.* London: Faber, 1977.

Bronfen, Elisabeth. *Over Her Dead Body: Death, Femininity, and the Aesthetic.* New York: Routledge, 1992.

Bronfen, Elisabeth, and Sarah Webster Goodwin, eds. *Death and Representation.* Baltimore: Johns Hopkins University Press, 1993.

Brontë, Charlotte. *Jane Eyre: An Authoritative Text, Backgrounds, Criticism.* Edited by Richard J. Dunn. New York: Norton, 1971.

———. "Editor's Preface." In *Wuthering Heights: Revised, an Authoritative Text with Essays in Criticism,* by Emily Brontë, edited by William M. Sale Jr., 9–12. New York: Norton, 1972.

———. *The Professor: A Tale.* New York: Harper, 1857.

———. *Villette.* Edited by Mark Lilly with an introduction by Tony Tanner. New York: Penguin, 1979.

Brontë, Emily. *Wuthering Heights: Revised, an Authoritative Text with Essays in Criticism.* Edited by William M. Sale Jr. New York: Norton, 1972.

Carlyle, Jane Welsh. *Letters and Memorials of Jane Welsh Carlyle.* Prepared for publication by Thomas Carlyle. Edited by James Anthony Froude. 3 vols. London: Longmans, Green, and Co., 1883.

———. *New Letters and Memorials of Jane Welsh Carlyle.* Annotated by Thomas Carlyle and edited by Alexander Carlyle with an introduction by Sir James Chrichton-Browne. London: John Lane, The Bodley Head, 1903.

Carlyle, Thomas. *A Carlyle Reader.* Edited by G. B. Tennyson. Cambridge: Cambridge University Press, 1984.

———. "The Hero as Poet. Dante; Shakespeare." In *Prose of the Victorian Period,* edited by William E. Buckler, 113–29. Boston: Houghton Mifflin, 1958.

———. "Labour." In *Past and Present,* edited by Richard Altick, 196–200. New York: New York University Press, 1977.

———. *Sartor Resartus.* Edited by Kerry McSweeney and Peter Sabor. New York: Oxford University Press, 1987.

Carpenter, Lynette, and Wendy K. Kolmar, eds. *Haunting the House of Fiction: Feminist Perspectives on Ghost Stories by American Women.* Knoxville: University of Tennessee Press, 1991.

Cecil, David. *Early Victorian Novelists: Essays in Revaluation.* London: Constable and Co., 1934.

Chambers, Robert. *Vestiges of the Natural History of Creation.* New York: Humanities Press, 1970.

Chapple, J. A. V. *Science and Literature in the Nineteenth Century.* London: Macmillan, 1986.

Chapple, J. A. V., and Arthur Pollard, eds. *The Letters of Mrs Gaskell.* Manchester: Manchester University Press, 1966.

Chase, Karen. *Eros and Psyche: The Representation of Personality in Charlotte Brontë, Charles Dickens, and George Eliot.* New York: Methuen, 1984.

Chitham, Edward. *A Life of Emily Brontë.* Oxford: Basil Blackwell, 1987.

Combe, George. *Notes on the United States of North America during a Phrenological Visit in 1838–9–40.* 2 vols. Philadelphia: Carey and Hart, 1841.

Cosslett, Tess. *Woman to Woman: Female Friendship in Victorian Fiction.* Atlantic Highlands, N.J.: Humanities Press International, 1988.

Cott, Nancy. *The Bonds of Womanhood: "Woman's Sphere" in New England, 1780–1835.* New Haven: Yale University Press, 1977.

Cottom, Daniel. *Abyss of Reason: Cultural Movements, Revelations, and Betrayals.* New York: Oxford University Press, 1991.

Cox, Michael, and R. A. Gilbert, eds. *Victorian Ghost Stories: An Oxford Anthology.* Oxford: Oxford University Press, 1991.

Craik, W. A. *Elizabeth Gaskell and the English Provincial Novel.* London: Methuen, 1975.

Crowe, Catherine. *Ghosts and Family Legends: A Volume for Christmas.* London: Newby, 1859.

———. *The Night Side of Nature; or, Ghosts and Ghost Seers.* 2 vols. Folcroft, Pa.: Folcroft Library Edition, 1976.

———. *Spiritualism and the Age We Live In.* London: Newby, 1859.

Cruikshank, George. *A Discovery Concerning Ghosts: With a Rap at the Spirit-Rappers.* London: Frederick Arnold, 1863.

Daly, Mary. *Pure Lust: Elemental Feminist Philosophy.* Boston: Beacon Press, 1984.

Darwin, Charles. *The Origin of Species: A Variorum Text.* Edited by Morse Peckham. Philadelphia: University of Pennsylvania, 1959.

Davies, John D. *Phrenology: Fad and Science; a Nineteenth-Century American Crusade.* New Haven: Yale University Press, 1955.

Davis, Christina. "Interview with Toni Morrison." In *Toni Morrison: Critical Perspectives Past and Present,* edited by Henry Louis Gates Jr. and K. A. Appiah, 412–21. New York: Amistad, 1993.

De Beauvoir, Simone. *The Second Sex.* Translated by H. M. Parshley. New York: Random House, 1974.

De Montlosier, François Dominique de Reynaud. *Des Mystère de la vie humaine.* 2 vols. in one. Brussels: Dumont et Compagnie, 1829.

De Morgan, Sophia. *From Matter to Spirit: The Result of Ten Years' Experience in Spirit Manifestations. Intended as a Guide to Enquirers.* London: Longman, Green, Longman, Roberts, and Green, 1863.

Dickens, Charles. *Hard Times.* New York: Penguin, 1969.

———. "The Signalman." In *The Signalman and Other Ghost Stories,* 1–13. Chicago: Academy Chicago Publishers, 1988.

Dickerson, Vanessa D. "The Ghost of a Self: Female Identity in Mary

Shelley's *Frankenstein.*" *Journal of Popular Culture* 27, no. 3 (winter 1993): 79–91.

Doyle, Arthur Conan. *The History of Spiritualism.* 2 vols. in one. New York: Arno Press, 1975.

Easson, Angus. *Elizabeth Gaskell.* London: Routledge and Kegan Paul, 1979.

Eliot, George. *Adam Bede.* Edited by Stephen Gill. New York: Penguin, 1980.

———. *Daniel Deronda.* Edited by Barbara Hardy. New York: Penguin, 1967.

———. *The Lifted Veil.* New York: Penguin, 1985.

———. *Middlemarch.* Edited by Gordon S. Haight. Boston: Houghton Mifflin, 1956.

———. *The Mill on the Floss.* Edited by A. S. Byatt. New York: Penguin, 1979.

———. "Prospectus of the *Westminster and Foreign Quarterly Review.*" In *George Eliot: Selected Essays, Poems, and Other Writings,* edited by A. S. Byatt and Nicholas Warren, 3–7. New York: Penguin, 1990.

———. *Romola.* Edited by Andrew Sanders. New York: Penguin, 1980.

———. *Scenes of Clerical Life.* Edited by David Lodge. New York: Penguin, 1973.

———. "Worldliness and Other-Worldliness: The Poet Young." In *Essays of George Eliot,* edited by Thomas Pinney, 335–85. New York: Columbia University Press, 1963.

Felman, Shoshana. *What Does a Woman Want? Reading and Sexual Difference.* Baltimore: Johns Hopkins University Press, 1993.

Feltes, N. N. "Phrenology: From Lewes to George Eliot." *Studies in the Literary Imagination* 1 (1968): 13–22.

Ffrench, Yvonne. *Mrs. Gaskell.* Denver: Alan Swallow, 1949.

Fuller [Ossoli], Margaret. *Woman in the Nineteenth Century, and Kindred Papers Relating to the Sphere, Condition, and Duties of Woman.* Edited by Arthur B. Fuller. Boston: Jewett, 1855.

Ganz, Margaret. *Elizabeth Gaskell: The Artist in Conflict.* New York: Twayne, 1969.

Gaskell, Elizabeth. *Cranford and Cousin Phillis.* Edited by Peter Keating. New York: Penguin, 1976.

———. *The Letters of Mrs Gaskell.* Edited by J. A. V. Chapple and Arthur Pollard. Manchester: Manchester University Press, 1966.

———. *The Life of Charlotte Brontë.* London: Dent, 1971.

————. *The Works of Mrs. Gaskell.* Edited and introduced by A. W. Ward. 8 vols. New York: AMS Press, 1972.

Gilbert, Sandra M., and Susan Gubar. *The Madwoman in the Attic: The Woman Writer and the Nineteenth-Century Literary Imagination.* New Haven: Yale University Press, 1979.

Gilmour, Robin. *The Victorian Period: The Intellectual and Cultural Context of English Literature, 1830–1890.* London: Longman, 1993.

Gissing, George. *New Grub Street.* Edited by Bernard Bergonzi. New York: Penguin, 1968.

Goldfarb, Russell M., and Clare R. Goldfarb. *Spiritualism and Nineteenth-Century Letters.* Cranbury, N.J.: Associated University Presses, 1978.

Gray, Beryl. Afterword to *The Lifted Veil,* by George Eliot. New York: Penguin, 1985.

Gray, B. M. "Pseudoscience and George Eliot's 'The Lifted Veil.'" *Nineteenth-Century Fiction* 36 (1982): 407–23.

Haight, Gordon S. *George Eliot: A Biography.* Oxford: Oxford University Press, 1968.

————, ed. *A Century of George Eliot Criticism.* Boston: Houghton Mifflin, 1965.

————, ed. *The George Eliot Letters.* 9 vols. New Haven: Yale University Press, 1954.

Haining, Peter, ed. *A Circle of Witches: An Anthology of Victorian Witchcraft Stories.* New York: Taplinger, 1971.

Hardinge [Britten], Emma. *Modern American Spiritualism: A Twenty Years' Record of the Communion between Earth and the World of Spirits.* New Hyde Park, N.Y.: University Books, 1970.

Hellerstein, Erna Olafson, Leslie Parker Hume, and Karen M. Offen, eds. *Victorian Women: A Documentary Account of Women's Lives in Nineteenth-Century England, France, and the United States.* Stanford: Stanford University Press, 1981.

Helsinger, Elizabeth K., Robin Lauterbach Sheets, and William Veeder. *The Woman Question: Society and Literature in Britain and America, 1837–1883.* 2 vols. Chicago: University of Chicago Press, 1983.

Hilgard, E. R. Introduction to *Mesmerism: A Translation of the Original Scientific and Medical Writings of F. A. Mesmer,* edited and translated by George Bloch. Los Altos, Calif.: William Kaufmann, 1980.

Holcombe, Lee. *Wives and Property: Reform of the Married Women's Property Law in Nineteenth-Century England.* Toronto: University of Toronto Press, 1983.

Houghton, Walter E. *The Victorian Frame of Mind, 1830–1870*. New Haven: Yale University Press, 1957.

Howitt, Mary. *Mary Howitt, an Autobiography*. Edited by Margaret Howitt. 2 vols. Boston: Houghton, Mifflin and Co., 1889.

Howitt, William. *The History of the Supernatural*. 2 vols. London: Longman, Green, Longman, Roberts, and Green, 1863.

Hughes, Winifred. *The Maniac in the Cellar: Sensation Novels of the 1860's*. Princeton: Princeton University Press, 1980.

Huxley, Thomas H. *On a Piece of Chalk*. Edited by Loren Eiseley. New York: Scribner, [1967].

Irigaray, Luce. *This Sex Which Is Not One*. Translated by Catherine Porter. Ithaca: Cornell University Press, 1985.

Jacobus, Mary. *Reading Woman: Essays in Feminist Criticism*. New York: Columbia University Press, 1986.

James, Henry. *The Turn of the Screw: An Authoritative Text, Backgrounds and Sources, Essays in Criticism*. Edited by Robert Kimbrough. New York: Norton, 1966.

Jameson, Anna. "Letter 142." In *Letters of Anna Jameson to Ottilie Von Goethe*, edited by G. H. Needler, 175. London: Oxford University Press, 1939.

Janouch, Gustav. *Franz Kafka und seine Welt*. Stuttgart: Hans Deutsch Verlag Wien, 1965.

Johnston, William. *England as It Is: Political, Social, and Industrial in the Middle of the Nineteenth Century*. 2 vols. Shannon, Ireland: Irish University Press, 1971.

Kaplan, Fred. *Dickens and Mesmerism: The Hidden Springs of Fiction*. Princeton: Princeton University Press, 1975.

———. "'The Mesmeric Mania': The Early Victorians and Animal Magnetism." *Journal of the History of Ideas* 35 (1974): 691–702.

Kerner, Justinus. *The Seeress of Prevorst, Being Revelations Concerning the Inner-Life of Man, and the Interfusion of a World of Spirits in the One We Inhabit*. Translated by Catherine Crowe. London: Moore, 1845.

Kerr, Howard. *Mediums, and Spirit-Rappers, and Roaring Radicals: Spiritualism in American Literature, 1850–1900*. Urbana: University of Illinois Press, 1972.

Knoepflmacher, U. C. *George Eliot's Early Novels: The Limits of Realism*. Berkeley: University of California Press, 1968.

———. "Thoughts on the Aggression of Daughters." In *The Endurance of "Frankenstein": Essays on Mary Shelley's Novel*, edited by George Levine and U. C. Knoepflmacher, 88–119. Berkeley: University of California Press, 1979.

La Belle, Jenijoy. *Herself Beheld: The Literature of the Looking Glass.* Ithaca: Cornell University Press, 1988.

Lang, Andrew. *Cock Lane and Common Sense.* New York: AMS Press, 1970.

Lansbury, Coral. *Elizabeth Gaskell: The Novel of Social Crisis.* New York: Harper and Row, 1975.

Laski, Marghanita. *George Eliot and Her World.* London: Thames and Hudson, 1973.

Leadbeater, C. W. *Clairvoyance.* Adyar, India: Theosophical Publishing House, 1903.

Le Fanu, Sheridan. "Green Tea." In *In a Glass Darkly,* edited by Robert Tracy, 5–40. Oxford: Oxford University Press, 1993.

Levy, Anita. *Other Women: The Writing of Class, Race, and Gender, 1832–1898.* Princeton: Princeton University Press, 1991.

Linton, Eliza Lynn. *Ourselves.* London: Chatto and Windus, 1884.

———, ed. *Witch Stories.* London: Chapman and Hall, 1861.

Marks, Patricia. *Bicycles, Bangs, and Bloomers: The New Woman in the Popular Press.* Lexington: University Press of Kentucky, 1990.

Marryat, Florence. *The Ghost of Charlotte Cray and Other Stories.* New York: Munro, 1884.

———. *The Spirit World.* Leipzig: Tauchnitz, 1894.

———. *The Strange Transfiguration of Hannah Stubbs.* Leipzig: Tauchnitz, 1896.

———. *There Is No Death.* New York: Lovell, Coryell and Co., 1891.

Martin, Emily. *The Woman in the Body: A Cultural Analysis of Reproduction.* Boston: Beacon Press, 1987.

Martineau, Harriet. *Miscellanies.* 2 vols. Boston: Hilliard, Gray, and Co., 1836.

———. *Miss Martineau's Letters on Mesmerism.* New York: Harper, 1845.

———. *Society in America.* New York: Saunders and Otley, 1837.

Martineau, Harriet, and Henry George Atkinson. *Letters on the Laws of Man's Nature and Development.* Boston: Mendum, 1851.

McVeagh, John. *Elizabeth Gaskell.* New York: Humanities Press, 1970.

McWhirter, David. "In the 'Other House' of Fiction: Writing, Authority, and Femininity in *The Turn of the Screw.*" In *New Essays on "Daisy Miller" and "The Turn of the Screw,"* edited by Vivian R. Pollak, 121–48. Cambridge: Cambridge University Press, 1993.

"Mesmeric Deceptions—The Whipton Prophetess." *Lancet* 1 (1847): 178–79.

Mill, John Stuart. *The Subjection of Women*. Cambridge: MIT Press, 1970.

———. "What Is Poetry?" In *Victorian Prose and Poetry*, edited by Lionel Trilling and Harold Bloom, 76–83. Oxford: Oxford University Press, 1973.

Mitchell, Sally, ed. *Victorian Britain: An Encyclopedia*. New York: Garland, 1988.

Moers, Ellen. *Literary Women*. Garden City, N.Y.: Anchor Books, 1977.

Moore, Katharine. *Victorian Wives*. London: Allison and Busby, 1974.

Morrison, Toni. *Beloved*. New York: Alfred A. Knopf, 1987.

———. *Song of Solomon*. New York: Alfred A. Knopf, 1977.

Myers, William. *The Teaching of George Eliot*. Totowa, N.J.: Barnes and Noble, 1984.

Nelson, Geoffrey K. *Spiritualism and Society*. New York: Schocken Books, 1969.

Oliphant, Margaret. *Autobiography and Letters of Mrs. Margaret Oliphant*. Edited by Mrs. Harry Coghill. Leicester: Leicester University Press, 1974.

———. *A Beleaguered City*. 1900; Westport, Conn.: Greenwood, 1970.

———. "Sensation Novels." *Blackwood's* 91 (1862): 564–84.

———. *Two Stories of the Seen and the Unseen*. Edinburgh: Blackwood, 1885.

Oppenheim, Janet. *The Other World: Spiritualism and Psychical Research in England, 1850–1914*. Cambridge: Cambridge University Press, 1985.

Orel, Harold. *The Victorian Short Story: Development and Triumph of a Literary Genre*. Cambridge: Cambridge University Press, 1986.

Owen, Alex. *The Darkened Room: Women, Power and Spiritualism in Late Victorian England*. Philadelphia: University of Pennsylvania Press, 1990.

Pater, Walter. *The Renaissance: Studies in Art and Poetry*. Introduction by Lawrence Evans. Chicago: Academy Press, 1977.

Patmore, Coventry. *The Angel in the House*. 4th ed. London: Macmillan, 1866.

Pearsall, Ronald. *The Table-Rappers*. London: Joseph, 1972.

Penzoldt, Peter. *The Supernatural in Fiction*. London: Peter Nevil, 1952.

Purkis, John. *A Preface to George Eliot*. London: Longman, 1985.

Pykett, Lyn. *Emily Brontë*. Savage, Md.: Barnes and Noble, 1989.

————. *The "Improper" Feminine: The Women's Sensation Novel and the New Woman Writing.* New York: Routledge, 1992.

Redinger, Ruby V. *George Eliot: The Emergent Self.* New York: Alfred A. Knopf, 1975.

Report on Spiritualism of the Committee of the London Dialectical Society, Together with the Evidence Oral and Written, and a Selection from the Correspondence. London: Longman, Green, Reader and Dyer, 1871.

Riddell, Charlotte. *The Collected Ghost Stories of Mrs. J. H. Riddell.* Edited by E. F. Bleiler. New York: Dover Press, 1977.

————. *The Uninhabited House.* In *Five Victorian Ghost Novels,* edited by E. F. Bleiler, 3–112. New York: Dover Press, 1971.

Roth, Ernest. *A Tale of Three Cities.* London: Cassell, 1971.

Russett, Cynthia Eagle. *Sexual Science: The Victorian Construction of Womanhood.* Cambridge: Harvard University Press, 1989.

Sargent, Epes. *Planchette; or, The Despair of Science. Being a Full Account of Modern Spiritualism, Its Phenomena, and the Various Theories Regarding It. With a Survey of French Spiritism.* Boston: Roberts Brothers, 1869.

————. *The Proof of Immortality.* Boston: Colby and Rich, 1875.

————. *The Scientific Basis of Spiritualism.* Boston: Colby and Rich, 1881.

Sawyer, Ruth. *The Way of Storytellers.* New York: Viking, 1953.

Schor, Hilary M. *Scheherezade in the Marketplace: Elizabeth Gaskell and the Victorian Novel.* New York: Oxford University Press, 1992.

Schor, Naomi. "This Essentialism Which Is Not One: Coming to Grips with Irigaray." In *Engaging with Irigaray: Feminist Philosophy and Modern European Thought,* edited by Carolyn Burke, Naomi Schor, and Margaret Whitford, 57–78. New York: Columbia University Press, 1994.

Schreiner, Olive. *The Story of an African Farm.* Edited by Joseph Bristow. Oxford: Oxford University Press, 1992.

————. *Woman and Labour.* Toronto: Henry Frowde, 1911.

Shelley, Mary. *Frankenstein, or the Modern Prometheus.* Edited by M. K. Joseph. London: Oxford University Press, 1969.

Shorter, Clement. *The Brontës: Life and Letters; Being an Attempt to Present a Full and Final Record of the Lives of the Three Sisters. . . .* 2 vols. New York: Haskell, 1969.

Showalter, Elaine. *A Literature of Their Own: British Women Novelists from Brontë to Lessing.* Princeton: Princeton University Press, 1977.

Shuttleworth, Sally. *George Eliot and Nineteenth-Century Science: The Make-Believe of a Beginning.* Cambridge: Cambridge University Press, 1984.

Sinclair, Marie, Countess of Caithness. *A Midnight Visit to Holyrood.* London: C. L. H. Wallace, 1887.

Spretnak, Charlene, ed. *The Politics of Women's Spirituality: Essays on the Rise of Spiritual Power within the Feminist Movement.* New York: Anchor Books, 1982.

Stevenson, Robert Louis. *Dr. Jekyll and Mr. Hyde.* New York: Bantam Books, 1981.

Stewart, Garrett. *Death Sentences: Styles of Dying in British Fiction.* Cambridge: Harvard University Press, 1984.

Stimpson, Catharine R. Foreword to *Independent Women: Work and Community for Single Women, 1850–1920,* edited by Martha Vicinus, ix–x. Chicago: University of Chicago Press, 1985.

Stockton, Kathryn Bond. *God between Their Lips: Desire between Women in Irigaray, Brontë, and Eliot.* Stanford: Stanford University Press, 1994.

Stoneman, Patsy. *Elizabeth Gaskell.* Bloomington: Indiana University Press, 1987.

Sullivan, Jack. *Elegant Nightmares: The English Ghost Story from Le Fanu to Blackwood.* Athens: Ohio University Press, 1978.

Summers, Montague. *The Geography of Witchcraft.* 1927. Reprint. London: Routledge and Kegan Paul, 1978.

Tayler, Irene. *Holy Ghosts: The Male Muses of Emily and Charlotte Brontë.* New York: Columbia University Press, 1990.

Tennyson, Alfred, Lord. *In Memoriam.* Edited by Robert H. Ross. New York: Norton, 1973.

Tuana, Nancy, ed. *Feminism and Science.* Bloomington: Indiana University Press, 1989.

Uglow, Jennifer. *Elizabeth Gaskell: A Habit of Stories.* New York: Farrar Straus Giroux, 1993.

————. Introduction to *Victorian Ghost Stories by Eminent Women Writers,* edited by Richard Dalby, ix–xvii. New York: Carroll and Graf, 1988.

Vogler, Thomas A., ed. *Twentieth Century Interpretations of "Wuthering Heights": A Collection of Critical Essays.* Englewood Cliffs, N.J.: Prentice-Hall, 1968.

Walker, Mary. "Between Fiction and Madness: The Relationship of Women to the Supernatural in Late Victorian Britain." In *That Gentle Strength: Historical Perspectives on Women in Christianity,* edited by Lynda L.

Coon, Katherine J. Haldane, and Elisabeth Sommer, 230–42. Charlottesville: University Press of Virginia, 1990.

Wallace, Alfred Russel. *Miracles and Modern Spiritualism: Three Essays.* London: Spiritualist Press, 1878.

Wechsberg, Joseph. *Prague: The Mystical City.* New York: Macmillan, 1971.

Whitehill, Jane, ed. *Letters of Mrs. Gaskell and Charles Eliot Norton, 1855–1865.* London: Oxford University Press, 1932.

Wickwar, J. W. *Witchcraft and the Black Art.* London: Herbert Jenkins, 1973.

Winsbro, Bonnie. *Supernatural Forces: Belief, Difference, and Power in Contemporary Works by Ethnic Women.* Amherst: University of Massachusetts Press, 1993.

Woolf, Virginia. *A Room of One's Own.* New York: Harcourt Brace, 1929.

Wright, Edgar. *Mrs. Gaskell: The Basis for Reassessment.* London: Oxford University Press, 1965.

INDEX